Other Titles by *Langaa* RPCIG

Francis B Nyamnjoh
Stories from Abakwa
Mind Searching
The Disillusioned African
The Convert
Souls Forgotten

Dibussi Tande
No Turning Back. Poems of Freedom 1990-1993

Kangsen Feka Wakai
Fragmented Melodies

Ntemfac Ofege
Namondo. Child of the Water Spirits

Emmanuel Fru Doh
Not Yet Damascus
The Fire Within

Thomas Jing
Tale of an African Woman

Peter Wuteh Vakunta
Grassfields Stories from Cameroon
Green Rape: Poetry for the Environment
Majunga Tok: Poems in Pidgin English
Cry My Beloved Africa: Essays on the postcolonial Aura in Africa

Rosemary Ekosso
The House of Falling Women

Peterkins Manyong
God the Politician

Ba'bila Mutia
Coils of Mortal Flesh

Kehbuma Langmia
Titabet and The Takumbeng

Ngessimo Mathe Mutaka
Building Capacity: Using TEFL and African languages as development-oriented literacy tools

Milton Krieger
Cameroon's Social Democratic Front: Its History and Prospects as an Opposition Political party, 1990-2011

Sammy Oke Akombi
The Raped Amulet
The Woman Who Ate Python
Beware the Drives: Book of Verse

Susan Nkwentie Nde
Precipice

Francis B Nyamnjoh & Richard Fonteh Akum
The Cameroon GCE Crisis: A Test of Anglophone Solidarity

Joyce Ashuntantang & Dibussi Tande
Their Champagne Party Will End! Poems in Honor of Bate Besong

John Percival
The 1961 Cameroon Plebiscite: Choice or Betrayal

Albert Azeyeh
Reussite Scolaire, Faillite Sociale: Généalogie mentale de la crise de l'Afrique Noire Francophone

CRY MY BELOVED AFRICA
Essays on the Postcolonial Aura in Africa
Peter Wuteh Vakunta

Langaa Research & Publishing CIG
Mankon, Bamenda

Langaa Research & Publishing CIG
Mankon, Bamenda
Publisher:
Langaa RPCIG
(*Langaa* Research & Publishing Common Initiative Group)
P.O. Box 902 Mankon
Bamenda
North West Province
Cameroon
Langaagrp@gmail.com
www.langaapublisher.com

Distributed outside N. America by African Books Collective
orders@africanbookscollective.com
www.africanbookscollective.com

Distributed in N. America by Michigan State University Press
msupress@msu.edu
www.msupress.msu.edu

ISBN: 9956-558-73-7

Peter Wuteh Vakunta 2008
First Published 2008

DISCLAIMER
All views expressed in this publication are those of the author and do not necessarily reflect the views of Langaa RPCIG.

DEDICATION

To the sung and unsung heroes of Africa: Patrice Lumumba, Nelson Mandela, Winnie Mandela, Albert John Lutuli, Walter Sisulu, Steve Biko, Peterson, Joe Slovo, Samora Machel, John Garang, Kwame Nkrumah, Ahmed Sékou Touré, Ken Saro Wiwa, Murtala Mohammed, Thomas Sankara, Ruben Um Nyobe, Albert Womah Mukong, Wangari Maathai, Wole Sonyinka, Bate Besong, Olufela Olusegun Oludotun Ransome-Kuti, Desmond Mpilo Tutu, John Fru Ndi, Kofi Annan and Ernest Ouandie.

ACKNOWLEDGEMENT

Grateful acknowledgement is made to the following publications in which these articles were first published: *Codesria Bulletin* (Dakar), Pan-African Visions(USA), *The Northern Times* (South Africa), *The Teacher* (South Africa), *Drum* (South Africa), *The Northern Monitor* (South Africa), *Cameroon Post* (Cameroon),and *Cameroon Life Magazine* (Cameroon).

My sincere thanks also go to the Cameroon Radio and Television Broadcasting Corporation (CRTV) for airing some of the material in these articles within the framework of my talk show program 'Better English'. Special thanks to the South African Broadcasting Corporation (SABC) as well as the Wisconsin Public Radio (USA) for giving me the opportunity to disseminate some of the ideas expressed in these essays to the public. Undoubtedly, a work of this magnitude would never have seen the light of day without recourse to the publications of precursors in the field. I hereby acknowledge my indebtedness to them all.

PREFACE

CRY, MY BELOVED AFRICA is a compendium of essays having as locus the continent of Africa. It comprises insightful observations on the politics, governmental systems, political economy, cultural practices, educational systems and natural phenomena that impact the lives of Africans. True to the tradition of French novelist Stendhal, the author intends this work to serve as a mirror that reflects the day-to-day living of the different peoples that inhabit the fifty-three odd nation-states in Africa. Hopefully, it would serve as a useful pointer not only to the goings-on in contemporary Africa but also to the relationship between Africa and the rest of the globe.

Each write-up is an entity sufficient onto itself, harboring a specific theme. The stories deal with life yesterday, today and tomorrow; with the powers-that-be and the downtrodden. In determining the order of presentation of the articles in this volume, the author has advertently avoided chronology. Many readers will want to turn first to one essay, the title of which intrigues them the most. Whether you peruse the articles in the order in which they appear or move about as your fancy dictates, you stand to gain from the abundance of information that the book holds in store for you. We hope that it will be commissioned to fulfill the didactic and informative functions it was meant to perform.

The didactic value of the book resides in its suitability to the young and the old. The language is clear and free of sophistry. College and university students with an interest in African politics, history, culture, anthropology and economy should find this collection a priceless research tool. The crafting of this book was motivated by the need to educate the global community on current affairs in Africa. It is the fervent hope of the author that its publication would meet this objective.

"We have experienced contempt, insults and blows, morning, noon and night because we were blacks." [Patrice Lumumba, First Prime Minister of the former Congo murdered at 36]

Table of Contents

The Trouble with Africa	*1*
A Nation at Risk	*11*
A Celebration of Diversity	*24*
False Start in Post-colonial Africa-	*26*
It's a Battlefield	*31*
Discourse on Gender in Africa	*33*
African Time and Other Africanisms	*47*
Manufacturing the Illusion of Freedom	*50*
Myth about Africa's Collective Amnesia	*55*
A Continent's Dirty Linen	*59*
Phantoms of the Past	*61*
Path to Rebirth	*63*
Hitler in Africa	*65*
Aporia: Africa`s Demo-Dictators	*67*
Africa's Tsunami	*73*
Rite of Passage or Unsafe Ordeal	*77*
Notes	*80*
Works cited	*82*

Chapter One
THE TROUBLE WITH AFRICA

All too often, talk about Africa revolves around pessimistic undertones: "A continent for the taking", "the lost continent", "the Dark Continent", "a continent at risk" and more. Why is this so? Has Africa reached a point of no return? Is the African continent really unredeemable? What could Africans at home and in the Diaspora do in order to salvage their continent? These are some of the burning issues that will be addressed in this article. The author argues that in order to rescue the continent of Africa from the likelihood of a socio-economic cataclysm, Africans at home and in the Diaspora are duty-bound to investigate the root causes of the morass in which Africa finds herself today.

Many factors, I believe, account for the chronic underdevelopment of Africa, some dating as far back as the colonial era. In his seminal work titled *How Europe underdeveloped Africa* (1982), Sir Walter Rodney shows clearly how Europe, over the last four hundred years, underdeveloped Africa. He illustrates beyond reasonable doubt that most of the ills that afflict Africa currently are actually colonial legacies. Apologists of the self-styled "civilizing mission" tend to argue that colonialism was not entirely a bane for the people of Africa. They contend that colonialism did some good to Africans. For example, they argue that Africans learned to read and write thanks to the introduction of literacy to Africa's our culture, good roads were built for Africans who hitherto, used bush paths to commute between villages, and so on.

This reasoning, persuasive as it may sound, is, in fact, spurious. The truth of the matter is that colonialism was a one-armed bandit just as the whole concept of the "civilizing mission" was a farce. As Obiechina (1975:7) puts it:

> Colonialism [...] is a practice not a theory. It is a historical process and not an abstract metaphysical notion. Above all, it is a relationship of power at the economic, political and cultural level.

It should be noted that colonialism was a practice shrouded in its own contradictions. As Césaire (1989:7) points out: "*Une civilisation qui ruse avec ses principes est une civilisation moribonde.*" [A civilization that plays foul with its own principles is moribund]. The colonizer attempts to obliterate everything from the memory of the colonized about his past and creates antipathy for the colonized person's own civilization and culture. Arguing along similar lines, Juneja (1995:4) observes:

> The colonizer destroys the past of the colonized by changing the frame of reference of history from the colony to that of his mother country. He distorts and disfigures the historical past of the colonized to his advantage.

Memmi (1965:102) echoes him when he contends that the "historical catalepsy of the colonized" helps the colonizer in propagating and perpetuating the myth of his racial superiority. This type of cultural racism, he asserts, makes the colonized hate his language, dress, techniques, value systems, social institutions, historical past, religion and practically everything that is not connected with the colonizer. Thus the "social panorama" of the colonized "is destructed, values are flaunted, crushed, emptied" (Fanon, 1967, 16-17). The question that begs asking at this juncture is what colonizers had in mind when they scrambled for Africa? How did they intend to grapple with the multiple cultures that exist in Africa? Did they conceive the incorporation of indigenous cultures into Western cultures? These are probably lame questions given that the quintessence of colonialism is cultural glottophagia, the practice whereby the fostering of indigenous cultures is stifled by the imperial power. Clearly, the development of the culture of the colonized was perceived as antithetical to the colonizing mission.

It should be noted that although colonial administrators built a few roads, schools, hospitals and clinics, these infrastructures were not intended to serve Africans. The roads they built, for instance, were meant to enable them to siphon raw materials from Africa to feed Western industries. The schools they built were meant to train administrative auxiliaries, semi-literate Africans, who assisted the colonial masters in local administration. Arguing along the same lines, Amadou Koné (1993:28) observes:

> On s'accorde généralement sur le fait que l'enseignement colonial a eu pour but essentiel de former des cadres subalternes nécessaires au bon fonctionnement du système colonial.
>
> [There is a general consensus on the fact that the colonial education system was meant to train essentially subalterns needed to ensure the smooth functioning of the colonial administration.]

Thus, it would be less than candid to claim that colonialism, the highest stage of imperialism, was conceived with the well-being of Africans in mind.

The discourse of colonization is of such crucial importance that many African writers have taken to fictionalizing it. In his novel *Crépuscule des temps anciens* (1962), Burkinabe writer Nazi Boni attempts to subvert the Euro-centric notion that colonialism was for the good of the colonized. He does so by bringing under the spotlight the nefarious effects of colonization on Africans. Boni clearly ascribes the destruction of African cultural institutions to the advent of European colonizers to Africa. The era in which this devastation was taking place is portrayed as the *"crépuscule des temps anciens"* [the dusk of good old days] because it was the time when indigenous institutions were being destroyed by the white colonizers. As Kyoore (1996:64) contends, "against this backdrop, Boni's interest in historicity enables him to depict accurately the consequences of [...] colonial rule and to reject the notion that colonialism was for the good of those who were subjected to it." In a similar vein, Kenyan writer Ngugi wa Thiong'o (1989:2) has postulated that "Imperialism is not a slogan. It is real; it is palpable in content and form and in its methods and effects." As a matter of fact, what was totted around as the "development of Africa" by colonialists was a cynical expression for the callous exploitation of Africa's material and human resources. During the many years of colonial rule in Africa, the continent was made to stagnate while the rest of the world made quantum leaps toward progress. There is no gainsaying the fact that people who lose power inevitably lose control over their own destiny. This is what happened to colonized Africans. Power determines the extent to which a people can survive as an entity. Being compelled to surrender one's power entirely to someone else constitutes a form of underdevelopment in itself. Colonialism dispossessed Africans of their power base. Colonial education was conceived to serve this particular purpose.

Education for the underdevelopment of Africa

Education is critical for the socio-economic development of every society. The irony of the colonial educational system in Africa is that it was designed to hamper the intellectual advancement of Africans. The most obnoxious characteristic of colonial education in Africa was its irrelevance to Africans. Colonial education did not match the realities of African societies. The main purpose of colonial education was to dehumanize and brainwash Africans into believing that one day they would be like their colonial masters in thought and deed. It was a system designed to create an identity crisis. Racism and white supremacist complexes perpetuated by colonial authorities made it impossible for Africans to benefit from the colonial educational system.

It should be noted that Africa was not an educational *tabula rasa* (blank slate) when the whites came. Pre-colonial Africa boasted great universities such as the AL-AZHAR University in Egypt (we are aware that Egyptian hieroglyphics existed long before the development of written cultures in Europe), the University of Fez in Morocco, the University of Timbuktu in Mali and many more. Scholars of African history have documented the fact that African languages had long existed in the written form before some European languages. Diop (1981:215), for instance, notes that "Black African language has been the oldest written language in the history of humanity." Sadly enough, Africa's academic and cultural institutions were callously demolished in the wake of colonization. This is a reality that cannot be refuted because it exists in historical documents. The claim that Westerners "brought" education to Africa is not only a fallacy; it is an insult. Regardless of the colonial myth of the "civilizing mission", the truth of the matter is that Europe did not bring light and civilization to the so-called Dark Continent. As Nigerian writer Chinua Achebe has noted:

> African people did not hear of culture for the first time from Europeans; that their societies were not mindless but frequently had a philosophy of great beauty, that they had poetry and, above all, they had dignity. It is this dignity that many African peoples all but lost during the colonial period, and it is this that they must now regain."(Quoted in Olaniyan and Quayson, 2007: 25).

All in all, colonial education was a simulacrum intended to foster the reign of subordination, exploitation and inferiority complex in Africa. This explains why during the entire duration of colonial rule in Africa, the colonialists did not deem it necessary to train indigenous physicians, engineers and other technocrats.

The worst calamity that befell Africans during the colonial era, to my mind, was the loss of their cultural values, dignity and self-identity. Thinking along similar lines, Amilcar Cabral has argued that to "dominate a nation by force of arms, is, above all, to take up arms to destroy, or at least to neutralize and paralyze its culture." (Quoted in Obiechina, 1975:8) Cabral notes that cultural imperialism was an integral part of the system of economic exploitation and political oppression of Africans. Put differently, cultural subjugation was a prerequisite for the economic and political domination of Africans.

I have the firm conviction that the prime responsibility of Africa's men and women of letters, and historians today remains that of helping Africans know who they are, enabling them to regain their lost dignity and identity by showing them through the medium of literary and historical books what they lost as a result of slave-trade and colonialism. It was not just slave-trade that sounded the death knell of Africa. Colonialism completed the havoc that European slave traders had started to wreak on the African continent. As Koné (op cit, 25) posits:

> La Traite des esclaves qui en deux siècles a vidé l'Afrique d'au moins une centaine de millions de ses habitants porte le premier coup grave aux temps héroïques et aux sociétés heureuses du continent noir. Elle désorganise et affaiblit les Etats, détruit les foyers artistiques naguères florissants et sème le doute dans l'âme de l'africain [...] La Traite semble avoir été pour les sociétés traditionnelles d'Afrique une grande catastrophe dont la signification pouvait être la même qu'une grande sécheresse ou une grande calamité naturelle.
>
> [Slave-trade which in the course of two centuries deprived Africa of at least one hundred million persons was the first fatal blow dealt to the hitherto heroic and contented people of Africa. It disorganized and weakened States, destroyed artistic resources that were flourishing in the past; created doubt in the minds of Africans [...] Slave-trade seems to have been for traditional African societies a huge catastrophe whose impact could be compared to that of a severe drought or big natural disaster.]

Interestingly, these legacies seem to linger in Africa long after political independence.

Colonial legacies in post-colonial Africa

Colonial shortcomings did not disappear with the advent of so-called independence in Africa. More than four decades after achieving political independence, many African leaders are still behaving like frightened kindergarten kids at the beck and call of their ex-colonial masters. Post-colonial Africa has virtually been hijacked by the G8 (Group of most Industrialized Nations). So widespread is the angst provoked by the economic felonies committed against Africa by the G8 that this group has been re-christened the "Group of International Robbers" by some Africans. How does one explain the fact that the price of a bag of cocoa-beans produced by a poor African farmer in Abidjan or Accra is determined in Paris or London? There is no better way of putting a continent in a straitjacket!

This observation raises the belabored question: have things really changed in Africa after decolonization? The answer is everyone's guess. Post-colonial African leaders have had the chance to speed up the development of their various countries by fighting for economic autonomy. Surprisingly, all but a few have thrown away the golden opportunity. Where their voices are supposed to be heard decrying the misdeeds of ex-colonial masters, they have remained surprisingly mute. Little wonder, Africa has remained the granary of France, Britain, and other meddlesome Western powers. To put this differently, African leaders have failed to meet the expectations of the people that elected them into public office. This is a pointer to the fact that internal factors have continued to contribute to the sorry state in which our continent finds itself at present. As I see it, Africa is beset by three major cankers: the sacralization of political power, corruption and misgovernment.

The Sacralization of Political Power

More often than not, abuse of power in Africa goes unpunished largely because Africans have the tendency to revere political leaders. In Cameroon, the common saying is: "*Le chef a toujours raison*" [The boss is never wrong.] This attitude has a cultural basis. In Africa, traditional rulers are viewed as untouchables. In fact, in many African communities, traditional leaders (fons, chiefs, kings, sultans, lamidos, etc) are seen as intermediaries between the living and the dead. In other words, these so-called natural leaders are perceived as immortals" sitting on the stool" of the ancestors and wielding unquestionable power over their subjects.

In many parts of Africa, the sacred role assigned to chieftains has been transferred to the political arena. The consequence of this is that abuse of power and dereliction of duty often go without consequences. This has resulted in the gross misappropriation of public funds, the proliferation of one-party governments or no-party "democracies" (the case of Uganda) and the emergence of "presidents for life" (e.g., late Kamuzu Banda of Malawi, Omar Bongo of Gabon, etc). The presidents of Cameroon, Zimbabwe, and Egypt are other cases in point. Late President Kwame Nkrumah of Ghana is known to have adopted the title of "Osagyefor" meaning "savior" or "redeemer" and actually approved of being treated as a demi-god during his tenure. Late President Ahmadou Ahidjo of Cameroon behaved in the same manner during his twenty-two-year presidency. He cherished the idea of being referred to as *"Le Père de la Nation"*, which could be translated as" Father of the Nation." Africans need to come up with a new modus operandi of political leadership and power-sharing for the betterment of Africa. Otherwise, multiparty politics and democracy will remain games to be played on an ethnic chessboard. Our brand of democracy has been contaminated by the germs of tribalism, cronyism and nepotism. Our elections have remained window-dressings as we continue to turn a blind eye to wanton abuse of power and corrupt practices.

Corruption: A Stumbling Block to Africa's Development

Corruption has been described by political science pundits as Africa's deadliest cancer. The prevalence of corrupt practices poses serious developmental challenges on the continent. It is a canker that is eating deep into the marrow of Africa's social fabric. Corruption from within has become more dangerous and destructive to nation-building than the forces of oppression from the outside. No longer is it possible to ignore corruption and the injustice it engenders in Africa. According to the findings of the Berlin-based, international watchdog, Transparency International (TI), post-colonial Africa is one of the worst victims of political corruption on the globe. This trend has to be reversed in order to give Africa the chance to develop. In spite of the abundance of natural resources in Africa: gold, crude oil, diamonds, bauxite, aluminum, copper, uranium, manganese, phosphates, iron ore, tin, limestone, coffee, cocoa, maize, cotton, wheat, rice, livestock, rubber, sorghum, timber, tea, fish to name but a few, Africa remains paradoxically the poorest continent on earth! This is an irony of sorts. Statistics indicate that a huge chunk of the gross national product of African countries is squandered through corrupt practices facilitated by tribalism, cronyism and nepotism.

Needless to say that corruption is not restricted to bribery. Corruption includes the illegal, unethical peddling of influence: big-time corruption. Extortion is another example of corruption existing in every African country. Other forms of corrupt practices are: graft, fraud, nepotism, kickbacks, favoritism and the misappropriation of state funds. I have to mention the petty corruption that prevails in Cameroon notoriously called *"gombo"* or *"tchoko"*. These are extortion practices where members of civil society or the armed forces, generally referred to as *"mange-mille"* [1] extort sums of money from people needing government services. This is practiced on a large scale nationwide. Corruption is a spoke in Africa's wheel of development. It hinders developmental initiatives throughout the continent. This problem is compounded by inept leadership.

Misgovernment in Africa

The sad thing about the African continent is that it is saddled with inept megalomaniacs, most of whom are lackeys of Western powers. Many reasons account for this state of affairs: inferiority complex, dependency syndrome, technical and technological deficiencies, and chronic indebtedness.

In most African countries, bullets have replaced ballots as instruments of governance. In quite a few countries, inter-tribal conflicts have degenerated into civil wars. What transpired in Rwanda, Burundi, Sierra Leone, Liberia, Sudan, Côte d'Ivoire, the Democratic Republic of the Congo (DRC), and most recently Kenya, is still fresh in our minds. In other words, the post-colonial dream of Africa has been shattered and transformed into a mirage!

These factors have far-reaching ramifications for the development of the African continent:
- African countries are debt-ridden (debt servicing consumes a considerable percentage of the national budgets in Africa);
- The development of Africa is impeded by structural adjustment programs imposed on nation-states by the Bretton Woods institutions (i.e., the International Monetary Fund and the World Bank).
- Stifling of domestic industries;
- Foreign interference in the internal affairs of African nation-states; and
- Bad governance (absence of transparency and accountability).

The question that must be asked at this point is whether there is any hope for Africa. This writer believes that there is light at the end of the tunnel. To achieve meaningful political and economic advancement, Africans have to think and come up with effective paradigms that would guarantee genuine economic freedom and sustainable development. The time has come for Africa to go beyond blaming the West for all her ills. Africa has to learn to take Africans to task for failing to live up to expectations. In other words, the accusing finger must now turn inward.

Conclusion

In order to salvage the African continent from socio-economic stagnation, Africans at home and in the Diaspora must take the following bold steps:
- Africans must take their destiny into their own hands by combating endemic corruption through moral education and the inculcation of life skills (truth, integrity, loyalty, respect, honesty, trustworthiness, patriotism) into citizens. No amount of good will is sufficient to resolve Africa's developmental problems. We have to learn to be our own nurses;
- Africans have to fight poverty by all means necessary, including redirecting educational expenditure toward the acquisition of skills needed in the workplace;
- Africans must foster South-South dialogue and encourage regional trade integration (build and sustain regional economic blocks amongst African countries) ECOWAS, SADC, NEPAD, are existing examples to emulate and improve upon. The New Partnership for Africa's Development (NEPAD) has been adopted as the continent's main developmental blueprint. According NEPAD officials, the attainment of Africa's long-term development goals is anchored in the determination of African peoples to extricate themselves and the continent from the malaise of underdevelopment. This requires a new type of relationship between Africa and the international community, in which Africa's economic partners will seek to complement Africa's developmental efforts. For Africa to achieve significant development, NEPAD has adumbrated three conditions that must prevail:
- Peace, security, democracy and good governance;
- Improved economic and corporate integration, and
- Regional cooperation and integration.

NEPAD has further identified several priority sectors requiring special attention and action:
- Physical infrastructure, especially roads, railways and power systems linking neighboring countries;
- Information and communication technology;
- Human development, focusing on health, education and skills development, and
- Promoting the diversification of production and exports.

In sum, in this piece, I have argued that Africa is neither a continent at risk nor one for the taking. She may be home to the world's most underprivileged people; she may be saddled with some of the deadliest endemic diseases on the globe, she may even be in the throes of underdevelopment. Regardless, she remains one of the most robust continents on the planet. No continent that I know of has ever been subjected to the same magnitude of exploitation, dehumanization, denigration, and brutality that have been the lot of Africa. Yet, in the face of all this, Africans have continued to hold their heads high, and to walk tall in the face of provocation. To forge ahead, Africans need to transform their hard-won political independence into genuine economic autonomy. We must learn to invest in the future because a saving continent is a prosperous continent. The journey toward de facto decolonization must begin with genuine economic liberation.

Chapter Two
A NATION A RISK

You may remember *Animal Farm*, the 1945 classic written by George Orwell. Many in my generation had to read this book in order to pass the General Certificate of Education (GCE) examination. Over the years I have come to see the relevance of the message in the novel even more as I ponder the Cameroon Anglophone Question.

The plot of the book is centered on the dissatisfaction of farm animals who felt they're being mistreated by Farmer Jones. Led by the pigs, the animals revolted against their oppressive master, and after their victory, they decided to run the farm themselves on egalitarian principles. However, the pigs became corrupted by power and a new tyranny was established. The famous line: "All animals are equal, but some animals are more equal than others" (92) still rings true to date. The socio-political status quo in Cameroon at present is a parody of *Animal Farm*. The novel is a replica of what has come to be referred to as the Cameroon Anglophone Question.

The Anglophone Question

After fighting together to decolonize Cameroon from French and British hegemony, French-speaking Cameroonians now tend to lord it over their English-speaking compatriots. There is no gainsaying the fact that there exists a generation of English-speaking Cameroonians who now find themselves at a crossroads and would like to know where they really belong. Many Anglophone Cameroonians are now asking themselves why they are condemned to play second fiddle in the land of their birth. The unfair treatment meted out to English-speaking Cameroonians by arrogant, condescending francophone compatriots in positions of power is a time bomb, I believe, that needs to be defused before it explodes to do irreparable damage. Unfair discrimination sows seeds of discord regardless of where it is practiced. Prejudice, in all its shades and colors, is deleterious in all parts of the world. A celebrated American literary icon, Maya Angelou (1986:5) once said: "Prejudice is a burden which confuses the past, threatens the future, and renders the present inaccessible."

The cohabitation between Anglophone and Francophone Cameroonians has been branded a marriage of convenience by scholars and students of post-colonial Africa. In fact, the uneasy co-existence between these two linguistic communities has been likened by some critics to the attitude of two travelers who met by chance in a roadside shelter and are merely waiting for the rain to cease before they continue their separate journeys in different directions. No other metaphor could better depict the frictional coexistence between Anglophone and Francophone Cameroonians.

More often than not, the perpetrators of this macabre game of divide and rule are the French-speaking political leaders who take delight in fishing in troubled waters. They divide in order to conquer to the detriment of the proverbial man in the street. In so doing, they stoke the flames of animosity and whip up sentiments of mutual suspicion between Anglophones and Francophones at the expense of nation-building. Many of them have been heard to make statements intended either to cow Anglophones into submission or to incite them into open rebellion. Yet these self-styled leaders would mount the podium to chant to the entire world that there is no Anglophone Problem in Cameroon. This type of hogwash, it seems to me, will come back to haunt them. Nemesis has uncanny ways of getting at its culprits. The plain truth is that there is a palpable feeling of discontent and dissatisfaction amongst Anglophones in Cameroon. Questions that remain unanswered are numerous: Are Anglophone Cameroonians enjoying equal treatment with their Francophone counterparts in the workplace? Are Anglophone Cameroonians having their fair share of the national cake? Do they feel at home in Cameroon? These and many more interrogations constitute what has been labeled the Cameroon Anglophone Question.

The Cameroon Anglophone Problem manifests itself in the form of complaints from English-speaking Cameroonians about the absence of transparency and accountability in matters relating to appointments in the civil service, the military, the police force, the *gendarmerie*[2] *and the* judiciary. In short, the Anglophone Problem raises questions about participation in decision-making as well as power-sharing in the country. This is not a figment of anyone's imagination! It is real, tangible and verifiable. The Anglophone Problem is the cry of an oppressed people, lamenting over the ultra-centralization of political power in the hands of a rapacious oligarchy based in Yaoundé, the nation's capital, where Anglophones with limited proficiency in the French language are made to go through all kinds of odds in the hands of cocky Francophone bureaucrats who look down on anyone speaking English. The Anglophone Problem stems from the supercilious attitude of French-speaking Cameroonians who believe that their Anglophone compatriots are unpatriotic, and therefore, should be asked to seek refuge in another country! This bigotry compounded by conceit has given rise to the rampant use of derogatory slurs such as" *les Anglophones sont gauches"*³, *"c'est des ennemis dans la maison"*⁴, *" ce sont les biafrais*⁵ and so on.

The consequence of this anti-Anglophone sentiment is the birth of the misconception that Anglophone Cameroonians are unreliable and untrustworthy, and therefore, undeserving of positions of leadership. This explains why key ministerial positions in Cameroon are the exclusive preserve of French-speaking Cameroonians. Such ministries include: Defense, Finance & Economy and Territorial Administration. Anglophobia has also led to the appointment of Francophones with no working knowledge of the English language to ambassadorial positions in strategic countries like the United States of America, Great Britain, Germany, Nigeria and South Africa where they wind up making a complete fool of themselves linguistically and culturally speaking. The presidency of the Republic and its ancillary organs are "no-go" zones for Anglophone Cameroonians. Although political appointments in this country ought to be done in conformity with the constitutional "regional balance paradigm", it is common knowledge that distrust of English-speaking Cameroonians has made the implementation of this constitutional stipulation a dead letter over the years. It should be noted that the relegation of Anglophone Cameroonians to the periphery in matters pertaining to political appointments has nothing to do with incompetence. In fact, the cream of Cameroon's intelligentsia are Anglophones thanks to the existence of world class Anglo-Saxon secondary schools such as Sacred Heart College-Mankon, St. Joseph's College-Sasse, Our Lady of Lourdes-Bamenda, CPC-Bali and a host of others that have churned out well-groomed administrators, scientists, technocrats, etc.

Sadly enough, the administrative system in Cameroon does not reward merit. In fact, the requiem for meritocracy was sung in this country the very day the colonizers left for Europe. Giving reward to those who deserve it has no signification in Cameroon. Corruption and nepotism are the yardsticks used in the selection of applicants to work in the civil service and other workplaces in this unfortunate geographical expression called *Ongola*⁶. Little wonder, the Berlin-based watchdog, Transparency International, has declared Cameroon one of the most corrupt nations in the world! In the same vein, **Marilyn Greene (2005:1), Press Fellow from USA,** in an interview with Jeff Ngwane Yufenyi in the November 23, 2005 edition of the *Post*, pointed out: **"Corruption is a plague affecting everyone from top government officials to poor folks in the street."** She made the statement in reaction to the outcry on corruption in Cameroon in Bamenda, at the opening of a two-day seminar on Media Excellence in Cameroon.

Corrupt practices affect the manner in which revenue from natural resources is used in Cameroon. Statistics indicate that about sixty percent of Cameroon's wealth in natural resources is located in the English-speaking part of the country. Yet the Francophone region takes the lion's share of the national budget intended for the building of roads, hospitals, schools and other social services. This state of affairs has been described by some critics as "jungle justice"! We are where we are today, saddled with the elephantine problem called the Anglophone Problem because of mutual misunderstanding amongst Francophone and Anglophone Cameroonians.

Open hostility toward Anglophones reached its acme many years ago when English-speaking Cameroonian students protesting against discrimination on the basis of the language of instruction at the University of Yaoundé went on strike and chanted the "We shall overcome" rallying song. Francophone members of government with limited proficiency in the English language accused them of singing the national anthem of a foreign country, Nigeria, and told Anglophones to go and live in Nigeria if they were not happy in Cameroon! In other climes, these officials would have been asked to resign without further ado. Never in Cameroon, where nonsensical statements like these actually earn accolades. How else can leaders show the world that they are square pegs in round holes?

In a similar vein, the clamor for the democratization of the political system in Cameroon has been branded by some narrow-minded francophones as an Anglophone-Bamileke[7] conspiracy to overthrow the government of President-for-life, Mr. Paul Biya Mbivodo. Political myopia is one of Cameroon's cancers! There have been unbridled attempts by French-speaking Cameroonians to whip up anti-Anglophone sentiments in order to score political points. The Cameroon GCE Board imbroglio that bred fire and brimstone in the early 1990s is a case in point. The saga to create a separate examination board for the General Certificate of Education Examination for Anglophones brought Cameroon to a virtual standstill because French-speaking Cameroonians could not fathom how Anglophone "underdogs" could have the temerity to demand equal treatment with their "overlords". Thus, there is no gainsaying the fact that the use of language is a divisive factor in the Republic of Cameroon.

The Language Question

The question of language policy in Cameroon is another bone of contention. There is no language policy, to the best of my knowledge, put in place to prevent the marginalization of linguistic minorities. The interpretation of the letter and spirit of the law is left to the whims and caprices of French-speaking judges who are ignorant of how the Anglo-Saxon judicial system works. This has resulted in several instances of miscarriage of justice in Cameroon. Miscarriage of justice was self-evident during the infamous Yondo Black trial way back in the 1990s when an Anglophone witness was deprived of his right to testify on the grounds that the presiding judge could not understand English. One wonders what has become of the pool of translators and interpreters who are vegetating at the Presidency of the Republic.

The Cameroon Radio & Television (CRTV) is another sore point. It has been so "french-fried"[8] that 95 percent of the programs are broadcast in French only, to the detriment of English-speaking Cameroonians. Programs in English obtained from overseas are rapidly translated into French to serve the needs of the Francophone majority at the expense of the Anglophone minority. The language of training and daily routine in the military, police and gendarmerie is French. Anglophones can go to Hades if they do not understand French! That's the state of affairs in that part of Africa called Cameroon! That is the Anglophone Problem in plain terms. There is no turning a blind eye to it. It will come back to haunt not just the present generation of Cameroonians but also those yet to be born. It may even affect Africa as a whole because Cameroon is, indeed, Africa in miniature. Trust me; it has happened elsewhere, it can happen in Africa. We've got to face it, and face it squarely. We don't need another Bosnia on the globe. Of all the burning issues that remain unresolved in Cameroon in the wake of independence, the language question is perhaps the thorniest. The imbroglio has degenerated into the well-known identity crisis amongst English-speaking Cameroonians, a crisis which this writer has captured in a poem titled "Identity Crisis":

    I don't quite know who I am.
    Je ne sais pas au juste qui je suis.
    Some call me Anglo;
    D'autres m'appellent Frog.
    I still don't know who I am
    Je ne sais toujours pas qui je suis.
    My name c'est Le Bamenda;
    My name is L'Ennemi dans la maison;
    My name c'est le Biafrais;
    Mon nom is underclass citizen;

>   My name c'est le maladroit.
>
>   Taisez-vous! Shut up!
>   Don't bother me!
>   Ne m'embêtez pas!
>   Don't you know that je suis ici chez moi?
>   Vous ignorez que I belong here?
>   I shall fight to my dernier souffle
>   to forge a real name pour moi-même.
>   You shall call me Anglofrog!
>   Vous m'appelerez Franglo!
>
>   Shut up! Taisez-vous!
>   Don't bother me!
>   Ne m'embêtez pas!
>   Vous ignorez que I belong here?
>   Don't you know que je suis ici chez moi?
>
>   I shall fight to my last breath
>   to forge a real lingo for myself.
>   I'll speak Français;
>   Je parlerai English
>   Together we'll speak camfranglais;
>   C'est-à-dire qu'ensemble,
>   We'll speak le Camerounisme,
>   Because ici nous sommes tous chez nous
>   A bon entendeur salut!
>   He who has ears should hear!⁹

More than forty years after accession to political independence, it is unimaginable that there is no reliable indigenous language policy in Cameroon. Unlike most other African countries which give pride of place to their indigenous languages, French and English, languages of colonial masters, remain the official languages of Cameroon in stark defiance of the national constitution which stipulates:

> The State shall guarantee the promotion
> of bilingualism throughout the country.
> It shall endeavor to protect and promote
> national languages (Article 1.3: 5)

Cameroon stands out as a sore finger in the African linguistic landscape. The question that begs asking here is why Cameroon, which boasts two hundred and thirty-six native tongues, does not have an official indigenous language policy. Why is it that we are still dressed in borrowed robes many years after independence? How can we talk of a Cameroonian national identity without an indigenous language policy? Are Cameroonian policy-makers oblivious of the fact that language conveys the culture of a people? Language does not only serve as the cultural repertory and memory-bank of a people, it is also an embodiment of both continuity and change in the historical consciousness of a community of speakers of the language. Each native language in Cameroon reflects the concerns, attitudes and aspirations of its speakers. In other words, our indigenous languages carry with them the habits, mannerisms, and identity of its native speakers. Don't Cameroonians have the right to articulate their own cultural identities? They cannot portray their cultural identities by speaking in foreign tongues; by bowing to assimilation. Bjornson (2001:19) has described assimilation in Africa as: "The adoption of European tastes, languages, customs, and colonial government policies by Africans." Arguing along similar lines, late Bob Marley once called on the colonized people of the world to reject mental slavery. Language is the soul of a people. Language transports culture. If you destroy a man's language, you have destroyed the man!

Sadly enough, Cameroonians relish borrowed cultures to the detriment of their indigenous cultures. We continue to speak in foreign tongues many decades after the departure of our banana-skin former masters! This is attributable, in the most part, to government lack of interest in promoting indigenous language education. Albert Gerard (1988:265) is right when he points out:

> [...]*Les gouvernements issus de l'empire français ne prennent guère de mesures efficaces pour encourager l'activité écrite dans les langues du peuple. Ils ont pour cela des motifs politiques valables.*
>
> [Governments that were formed in the wake of political independence from France do not take effective measures to foster the codification of indigenous languages. They have valid political reasons for not doing so.]

This leaves me with the irksome feeling that we have not yet liberated ourselves from mental slavery. Is it not true then that a true slave is not the one in chains? The acculturation that has taken deep root in Cameroon has had as a corollary the denigration of our traditional values. How many times have you heard mind-boggling comments like *"this man na kontry, he no sabe tok gramma"*[10] in reference to someone who strives to promote his mother tongue by speaking it as often as he can? Confiant et al. (1990:80) perceive this self-abnegation as an anomaly and points out that the tragedy of the colonized is the servile manner in which he tries to "portray himself in the color of elsewhere." Franz Fanon (1964:15) describes Africans who behave in this manner as people having "black skin" but wearing "white masks." There is no denying the fact that a man who wields his language adeptly is culturally richer than he that doesn't. To fight cultural imperialism, it is incumbent on Cameroonians to defuse what Ngugi wa Thiongo (1986:3) calls the "cultural bomb". He maintains:

> [...] But the biggest weapon wielded and actually daily unleashed by imperialism against that collective defiance is the cultural bomb. The effect of a cultural bomb is to annihilate a people's belief in their names, in their languages, in their environment, in their heritage of struggle, in their unity, in their capacities and ultimately in themselves."

Language experts have pointed out that multilingualism is indispensable in today's global village. In fact, monolingualism, they argue, is now an anachronism in the contemporary multilingual societies in which we live. Bilingualism is an added advantage to the bilingual individual and to the nation as a whole given that what is acquired in one language is transferable to the second language. This is an enriching acquisition. It broadens the mindset of individuals in the linguistic community, and lubricates social intercourse. Studies have shown that multilingual individuals exhibit a higher degree of cognitive ability than monolinguals. Surprisingly, Cameroon's bilingual educational project has proven to be a nonstarter on account of tribal hostility and bigotry. The linguistic question is an offshoot of the animosity that separates Anglophones from Francophones in Cameroon. Revolting disdain for the English language has led French-speaking Cameroonians to downplay the use of English as an official language although the constitution of the Republic is explicit:

> The official languages of the Republic of Cameroon shall be English and French, both languages having the same status (Article 1.3: 5).

It needs to be pointed out that the second fiddle role that has been assigned to English-speaking Cameroonians by French-speaking members of government has made the implementation of the nation's bilingual education program a stillborn. There seems to be a deliberate attempt on the part of Francophone Cameroonians to undermine and eventually destroy the Anglo-Saxon culture in Cameroon. How does one explain the fact that in typical English-speaking towns and cities in Cameroon such as Buea, Tiko, Kumba, Bamenda, Bali, Nso and Nkambe to name but a few, one finds billboards with inscriptions written in French only? Tiko, a town in the South-West province is a good example. As one approaches this town, one is greeted by a billboard that reads: "Halte Péage!" For goodness sake, what does this mean to the Anglophone South-Westerner? How do the powers-that-be expect the average man who has never been exposed to French to understand what this inscription means? The case of Tiko is not an isolated one. There are myriads of such nonsensical billboards here and there throughout the national territory.

Similar linguistic hotchpotch litters airports throughout the country. The Nsimalen Airport in Yaoundé is an example. At Nsimalen commuters are able to read stomach-churning gibberish such as: "To gather dirtiness is good." This is a word-for-word rendition of the French: "ramasser la saleté c'est bien." The French in this sentence leaves much to be desired. But it is even more annoying to realize that there is no English language translation of the notices posted on the billboards. The creators of this unintelligible stuff know very well that in bilingual countries the world over, all official communication: billboards, memos, letterheads, road-signs, application forms, court forms, police documents, health forms, driver's licenses and hospital discharge forms are all written in the official languages of the country in question. Failure to do so is tantamount to a violation of the constitution, an illegal act punishable by law in any country where there is rule of law.

I have no doubt at all that diplomats accredited to Yaoundé and other foreigners who visit Cameroon find our official language policy and its implementation utterly ludicrous. One also finds on billboards inanities such as: "Not to make dirty is better". This incomprehensible trash is meant to be a translation for: "Ne pas salir c'est bien." If the situation were not so grave one would be laughing but the language question in Cameroon brooks no laughter.

Public authorities: mayors, governors, divisional officers, police officers and gendarmes are expected to maintain zero tolerance in upholding Cameroon's bilingual policy. Breaches of official language policies ought to be punished. It should be noted that there is a pool of translators and interpreters at the Presidency of the Republic spending time on trivialities. Why not use them to perform this important task? These technocrats who were educated at the expense of the taxpayer should be made to serve the nation by translating official documents aimed at public consumption. Administrators should avail themselves of the services of these well trained professionals. Let myopia, bigotry and blind allegiance not deter them from valuing the priceless work that translators and interpreters are capable of doing for the nation.

Personally, I couldn't care less how much cosmetic surgery French-speaking Cameroonians want to perform on the language of Voltaire. As a matter of fact, psycho-sociological factors have made me totally callous to the mastery of Voltaire's mother tongue beyond the ability to ask for water to drink when I am on a visit to the world of *La Francophonie*.[11] If I have acquired a smattering of French it is because it enables me to put an additional loaf of bread on the dinning table. What I do care very much about, though, is the place my mother tongue, *Bamunka*, occupies in the linguistic landscape in the land of my birth. It is the duty of each and every Cameroonian to prevent the demise of his or her own indigenous language, the more so because language abuse has become the hallmark of formal education in Cameroon. The importance of indigenous languages has been stressed by scholars in the field. It is noteworthy to point out the views of Nkrumah on the restoration of autochthonous languages as an indispensable part of our heritage. In his speech "Ghana is Born", Nkrumah saw the use of European languages in Africa as one of the problems compromising the freedom, equality and independence of African countries. He thus suggested the following blueprint:

> It is essential that we do consider seriously the problem of language in Africa[...] Far more students in our universities are studying Latin and Greek than studying the languages of Africa. An essential of independence is that emphasis must be laid on studying the living languages of Africa for, out of such a study will come simpler methods by which those in one part of Africa may learn the languages in all other parts.(Quoted in Kwame Botwe-Asamoah,2001:747)

In his discourse, Nkrumah not only saw the danger in neglecting one's mother tongue, but he also underscored the significance of the linguistic factor in African unity, the more so because as Ngugi (1986:13)has pointed out, "Every language has a dual makeup; it is both a mode of communication and a bearer of culture." Asante (1988:4) is probably right when he claims that "If your God cannot speak your language, then he is not your God."

Years ago, I read some material that lent credibility to Nkwumah's charge of linguistic abuse in Africa. The offensive document that I read was the C.A.P examination in Cameroon. The following is an excerpt culled for Francis Nyamnjoh's (1996:114) book:

> Each candidat should pick by bilot a
> sujet. Each sujet is mark over 40 marks.
> For each port, candidat shall establish
> the working mothed card. Fill in the
> analysis car in annexe B.

Honestly any one in his right mind reading this except should be wondering what on earth is going on in Cameroon. One wonders how Anglophone learners are expected to succeed in an examination in which the phraseology of the questions has been tinkered beyond intelligibility. The unintelligible stuff cited above was meant to serve as an examination that would determine the fate of thousands of Anglophone students who had spent four years studying at technical colleges nationwide. Little wonder they fail in drones. The good thing about this conundrum is that Anglophone parents and teachers are not willing to allow this sort of linguistic bastardization to go on forever. This rape of the English language speaks volumes about the disrespect Francophone educators and decision-makers have for English-speaking Cameroonians. When the senile Minister of National Education, Robert Mbella Mbappe, was confronted by some irate Anglophone parents and teachers over the nature of this examination as well as the need for an independent Examination Board for Anglophones, here is the response he gave to the representatives of TAC and the SONDENGAM Commission: "You can do whatever you like with your so-called GCE board, none of my children studies in Cameroon." (Op cit, 114)

Hard to believe that this is the Minister of National Education, paid by the taxpayer, literally spitting in the face of the same taxpayer! In another country, he would have been asked to step down from his position without ceremony.

Conclusion

In this piece, I have endeavored to pinpoint the root causes of the so-called Cameroon Anglophone Question. It is a problem, I believe, that harbors far-reaching implications for the socio-economic development of the nation. It would amount to living in fool's paradise to dismiss the legitimate complaints of English-Speaking Cameroonians as the ranting of a few disgruntled individuals as some French-speaking Cameroonians have claimed. When all is said and done, we must ask ourselves the inevitable question: Is there light at the end of the tunnel in Cameroon? The response is in the affirmative. What needs to be done, in my opinion, is to cease acting the ostrich, and take giant steps toward addressing the issue by all means necessary. If convening a national conference would serve this purpose, I see no reason why Cameroonians should not be given the opportunity. Cameroonians are living in what some perspicacious observers have termed the "post-independence time-bomb". In other words, post-colonial Cameroon has gotten to a point where many are wishful about the days before the departure of the white man! In order to salvage this enviable country from the canker of corruption, unfair discrimination, false pretenses, bad governance, and tribalism Cameroonians at home and overseas must take a number of realistic measures:

- Cameroonians have to get rid of the colonial mentality and assume the posture of architects of their own destiny. The belief that international goodwill will solve our developmental problems is a fallacy. We must be prepared to look one another in the face and say: look, this is where we went wrong; it is time to correct the mistakes of the past and move on toward seeking long-lasting solutions to prevalent problems in our country;
- They must combat corruption in all its forms;
- They have to fight poverty, including intellectual poverty by all means necessary. This means redirecting economic resources toward the acquisition of much-needed skills;
- They must make assure that their hard-won political independence is not a sham. To put this differently, political independence must be backed by economic freedom. This is the point Ngwane (2004:14) underscored when he wondered: "Of what use is political freedom without economic emancipation?"

Ngwane's question is not an idle one. Nearly fifty years after independence, it is a shame to realize that Cameroon is still tied to the bootstraps of France, in every sense imaginable. Cameroon should be in a position to assert itself and conceive a framework that would lead her toward peace and prosperity.

- Most importantly, Cameroonians need an able leadership. The people that govern us today are "absentee landlords" with no vision at all. Under an enlightened leadership endowed with goodwill, Cameroonians should be able to harness their natural and human capital to serve all Cameroonians regardless of ethnic origin, creed, language, sexual orientation or gender.

All in all, I argue that Cameroon is not on the brink of collapse on account of its internal problems. I further contend that Cameroon has the potential to serve as Africa's success story provided Cameroonians are willing to sink their linguistic and cultural differences to work in tandem for the betterment of all and sundry. It has all that it takes to be the "bread basket" Africa. To attain this goal, Cameroonians must learn to rise above their petty tribal differences and see themselves first and foremost as citizens of one country. In the words of Ngugi (1986:3): "They must discover their various tongues to sing the song: 'A people united can never be defeated.'"

Chapter Three
A CELEBRATION OF DIVERSITY

The capacity to embrace diversity has always been part and parcel of the African mindset. Our cultures melt and spread into subcultures which in turn generate aggregates. In a bid to forge a common cultural identity and avoid asphyxiation, Africans have the onerous task of embracing their disparate subcultures. The submersion of our various cultures into a collective African heritage by means of mutual acceptance is one of the extraordinary ways in which Africans could enter into symbiotic intercourse with their kith and kin of different extractions. This is a rewarding means to communion with members of the global village. Our emotional experiences, our pains and our uncertainties, the strange curiosity of what is generally perceived as our defects and shortcomings should serve as a support base for our convivial strive toward a common identity.

One of the prerequisites for the collective survival of Africans is our ability to maintain a conscious relationship with one another and with the global community in which we live. This presupposes sinking our superficial differences and embracing our all too obvious commonalities. We must ensure that our collective consciousness celebrates and enrich rather than alienate us as a people from the community of nations. We constitute an integral part of the international community. Our African heritage should not be hijacked by others to place us in a pariah state. Our collective diversity should be perceived as part of an integrating process of world diversity. Africans must acknowledge that each culture is never a finished product but rather a rung in the continuum of global cultures. Africans are interested in relating rather than dominating, in exchanging rather than expropriating. That's why we remain our brother's keepers at all times. A Hausa from Nigeria is a brother to a Hausa in Cameroon. A Fulani in Chad is a sister to a Fulani in Niger, a Bororo from Gabon is kith and kin to a Bororo from Equatorial Guinea, and so on and so forth.

Without denying the cosmetic differences that exist amongst us, differences which have been exploited by our enemies to their own advantage, we must acknowledge that what unites us as Africans is vaster that what separates us. This is to say that the celebration of our diversity should constitute a stage in the process toward an African Federation, or better yet, the United States of Africa, the only contraption that will enable us to stand united. As the adage goes, united we stand; separated we will fall. Our unity will empower us to face up to the different hegemonic challenges that threaten our very survival in a global community that has become the marketplace for the commercialization of ideas.

Chapter Four
FALSE START IN POSTCOLONIAL AFRICA

The African continent has been described as a medley patchwork of disparate ethnic groups lumped together for the administrative convenience of imperial powers. This has meant doom for Africans. In his celebrated work titled *False Start in Africa* (1969:5) French agronomist René Dumont tells that story of post-colonial Africa. As he puts it, it is a tale of failure; failure on the whole due to the historical framework in which liberation has taken place. As he observes:

> The bewildering violence of the 'winds of change' in Africa has converted the most universally colonial continent into the greatest jumble of independent states. Their existence is in most cases due neither to the exigencies of geography nor ethnic unity. They are the ultimate results of the disastrous rivalry and the chase for colonial aggrandizement of the 'great powers' at the end of the nineteenth century. They are also the inheritors of the imperial institutions, especially in administrative structure and education, which suddenly lost such socio-economic relevance as they had never possessed.

Dumont's reasoning is that African nation-states as they exist today are the handiwork of outsiders, the treasure-seeking ex-colonial masters. Post-colonial Africa, he argues, took the wrong step right from the outset and has either been unwilling or too slow to correct lingering mistakes. Arguing long the same lines, Kambudzi (1995:10) notes: "The 'national question' has not been realistically and broadly regarded after independence." He further points out that at independence Africans glossed over crucial developmental questions and issues and stampeded into the bandwagon of post-colonial euphoria. He observes:

> Even the meanings of the post-colonial state and society, of development plans, of nation-building and nationalization have only been sought on the periphery of the hearsay of politicians, charismatic individuals and less committed individuals.

The truth of the matter is that post-colonial nation-states in Africa continue to hang in the balance. They have not gained economic independence from erstwhile colonial masters. As Dharam (1973:9) points out:

> [...] Despite the potency of the idea of economic freedom in shaping the goals and policies of numerous developing countries, very little intellectual effort has been expended in analyzing the concept and exploring its ramifications in the realms of politics, economics or sociology.

The reasons for this state of affairs are legion. Primarily, African nation-states are incapacitated by the economic morass in which they find themselves on account of being literally tied to the apron strings of erstwhile colonial overlords: Anglophone countries to Britain; Francophone countries to France, Lusophone countries to Portugal, etc. Dharam (1973:10) maintains that economic freedom "is defined to consist in the freedom of choice of economic agents, be they producers, consumers, employees or employers." Secondly, despite the fact that the colonial state has been replaced by independent African states, European money-capital still proposes and disposes in the era of neo-colonialism. As Obiechina (op cit) has observed, Europe has thrived on the brutal exploitation of Africans. The entire structure of power relationship between the colonizer and the colonized in Africa brings into the limelight the intertwinement of economics and politics.

The economic dependence of Africa on the West seems to spell doom. When politicians and economists talk of economic dependence, Dharam asserts, they may be referring to some or all of the following features of their economies:

- Structural characteristics of production and trade;
- Foreign aid and private capital flows form a high proportion of both public and total investment in the country;
- The share of foreigners in both the stock of capital in the modern sector and of skilled manpower is high; as a consequence of this, the foreign share in gross domestic income is high.

It is perturbing to realize that several years after gaining political independence from France, the economic policies of francophone African countries remain carbon copies of policies conceived to serve the economic interests of France. This holds true for the so-called Commonwealth countries who have remained minions to Britain. The reality is that *Francophonie*, the European Union, the Commonwealth and other Western economic blocks interested in Africa are merely paying lip service in order to rip Africa of her natural resources. It is time to change this trend. African countries, to my mind, will make or mar. Africa must desist from being inveigled into believing that the West is interested in her economic wellbeing. It is a misconception! Africans must stop thinking that financial aid is a panacea for Africa's developmental problems. We don't need aid; what we need is trade cooperation on a par with our trade partners. African governments need to do more than daydream and make empty promises. It is time for our leaders to get rid of what I see as the 'dependency complex' of post-colonial African nation-states. Put differently, it is incumbent upon Africans to stop feeling that somehow the African continent is tied to the umbilical cord of the West. We have to fully shoulder the responsibility for our own self-determination.

The ineptitude of the African middle-class is of such grave concern that Senegalese writer Sembène Ousmane has satirized it in his novel *Xala* (1973). This novel depicts third world bourgeoisie as people who are incapable of generating their own ill-gotten wealth through industrial expansion; instead they live as parasites in a neo-colonized society. "Xala" means "impotence" in Wolof, an allegorical reference to the inability of the African middle-class to extricate the continent from economic morass. Sembène uses his fiction to speak out on Africa's socio-political problems. He places emphasis upon ideological solutions to Africa's problems.

The way forward for Africa's socio-economic survival has been spelled out by the New Partnership for Africa's Development (NEPAD), brainchild of architects of the African Union (AU). NEPAD sessions should serve as forums for Africa's think-tanks to converge and rethink sound economic policies for the continent. It would be sad if such encounters were transformed into the same 'talk-shops' to which the now defunct Organization for African Unity (OAU) had accustomed us. Africans should work in concert toward consolidating regional trade arrangements (RATs). It is consoling to know that Africa is home to some 30 regional trade arrangements at the moment, many of which are part of bigger regional integration schemes.

Over and above, regional and sub-regional trade blocs, namely, the African Economic Community (AEC), Economic Commission of West African States(ECOWAS), the Southern African Development Community (SADC), Southern African Customs Union(SACU), East African Community (EAC),Preferential Trade Area for Eastern and Southern African States(PTA, Common Market for Eastern and Southern Africa(COMESA) and the Union Douanière et Economique de l'Afrique Centrale (UDEA)[Customs and Economic Union of Central Africa] should work in tandem to promote free trade agreements (FTAs) which would involve not only the removal of trade barriers (e.g., tariffs) but also the elimination of other stumbling blocks to the free movement of capital, goods and services on the African continent. Once this is done, I believe, Africa will not only experience a new lease of life but will be able to lay claim to genuine economic autonomy. It may be of some interest at this juncture to dwell on some of the parameters that would account for economic independence in Africa as discussed by Dharam:

- The substitution of national for foreign enterprises;
- A massive training program for the production of requisite workplace skills;
- Replacing foreign with national capitalists;
- The incorporation of a national element in foreign corporations;
- Encouraging the growth of indigenous entrepreneurship.

As one would imagine, there are many socio-politico-economic implications involved in the implementation of the aforementioned initiatives into which we cannot go here; but, as Dharam has noted, "[…] they invest the political and bureaucratic elite with immense powers to control the disposition of valuable resources." (op cit, 26)

In this essay, I have attempted to diagnose the causes of Africa's economic ailments. I have pointed out some of the pressing issues that need to be addressed in a bid to put the African continent back on a sound economic recovery track. I contend that the factors that account for the economic quagmire in which Africa finds her at present are both endogenous and exogenous, including neo-colonialism, lethargy toward finding lasting solutions to perennial problems, incessant meddling of Western powers in the internal affairs of Africa's nation-states, and collusion of the national bourgeoisie with the bourgeoisie of the metropole. The national bourgeoisie and comprador elites have compromised themselves by collaborating with foreign post-colonial forces to undermine African independence. It is no longer a secret that when the new African ruling and dominant elite ensure continued control of the management of national wealth by external Western financiers, they compromise the economic freedom of their respective countries. Africa has been usurped and vandalized by these inimical forces. The task of ridding Africa of this double yoke of external and internal exploitation is enormous. The anti-neo-colonial struggle is essentially an economic and political vendetta. It is also a struggle, I think, to be waged at the level of culture, values and attitudes. I have further noted that the quest for self-determination and South-South cooperation constitute effective recipes for Africa's economic liberation.

Chapter Five
IT'S A BATTLEFIELD

A cursory look at current events on the African continent leads one to scream like Graham Greene did many years ago in his book titled *It's a battlefield (1962)*. The title of his work brings to mind the telltale history of Africa. Ours seems to be a tale of violence and bloodshed. One only needs to take a walk down memory lane: the genocide in Rwanda and Darfur, the bloodbath in the Democratic Republic of the Congo, Liberia and Sierra Leone, the Saga in Côte d'Ivoire, and the recent ethnic cleansing that came in the wake of rigged elections in Kenya to name but a few. Many factors account for this impasse, the most patent of which are artificial boundaries created between African peoples by colonial masters. As Kambudzi (op cit, 8) posits:

> The irony with Africa is that its political boundaries derived from externally negotiated settlements, not to say brute European military force, rather than any ethno-linguistic arrangement.

The trail of economic destruction and human suffering left on the African continent by civil wars is without precedence. Why civil wars continue to be routine on our continent remains a moot point. One reason may be that political oppression, racial subordination and economic exploitation have condemned Africans to a common misfortune. Another reason for the recurrence of civil strife in Africa is that aspirants to political power have often held different views as regards new socio-politico-economic dispensations in their respective countries. Sometimes a civil war erupts as a result of the demise of a dictatorial political order under a tyrannical president. The case of the Somali civil war which erupted in the aftermath of the fall of the dictator, Siad Barre, is still fresh in our minds. The civil war that engulfed Liberia following the demise of Machiavellian Samuel Doe is another case in point. We cannot forget the civil war in Ethiopia that ended after the fall of Mengistu Haile Mariam.

In the main, it makes sense to conclude that the absence of a firm constitutional blueprint in the majority of African states has contributed immensely to the prevalence of civil wars on the continent. A firm constitutional blueprint would serve a two-fold purpose. Firstly, it would guarantee fair power-sharing and equitable participation in the political life of nations. Secondly, a good blueprint would ensure that there is organized political succession, including the formulation of laws that stipulate the terms of office for presidents, members of parliament and ministers. Nigeria embodies the political difficulties that Africa has experienced due to the absence of a constitutional framework. Despite the proliferation of constituent federal units in Nigeria, the conception of a firm constitutional and political order is still problematic. In consequence, the military has monopolized power in Nigeria since independence from Great Britain more than forty years ago. In the words of Kambudzi (op cit, 11),"Nigeria oscillates today between political chaos and military autocracy!" He describes Nigeria as a prototype of neo-colonial states characterized by the following ills:

- Foreign domination;
- Foreign ownership of big business;
- External military reinforcement;
- External financial control;
- Local intelligence services involving outside secret agents and mercenaries;
- Network of corruption; and
- Insignificant indigenous involvement in politics or business.

It has to be noted that the constitutional issue in Africa means more than simply drawing up a constitution. Africa's constitutions must be upheld in the day-to-day governance of nations. At present, there is too much toying around with national constitutions in Africa. There must be a way of holding African leaders accountable for any breaches of the constitution. The recent political fiascos in Togo and Cameroon are incontrovertible evidence that when the supreme law of the land is subjected to the whims and caprices of dishonest, self-seeking politicians, the end product is chaos and civil strife. Social stability and economic development are not chance occurrences. They are the result of sound decision-making.

By and large, the truth about Africa is that we are peace-lovers. Africans want a better place to live in. Sadly enough, when one looks at the history of Africa keenly, one observes three levels of oppression that stand out like sore fingers: blacks oppressing blacks, Arabs oppressing Blacks and whites (neo-colonizers) oppressing both Blacks and Arabs. We cannot allow this inhumane status quo to go on forever. The onus is on us all to devise ways and means to reverse the current trend.

Chapter Six
DISCOURSE ON GENDER IN AFRICA

Pregnant, bare-foot, and in the kitchen! This is the portrait of the legendary African woman. In his novel titled *Monnè: outrages et défis (1990:135)* Ivorian writer, Ahmadou Kourouma bemoans the fate of the African woman in the following terms: *"Dans ce monde, les lots de la femme ont trois noms qui ont la même signification: résignation, silence, soumission."* [There are three words for women's lot in this word and they all have the same meaning: resignation, silence, submission.]

This writer argues that a community that continues to relegate some of its members to the fringe of society is a community at risk. Interestingly, this is happening in most countries on the African continent where the woman's body has become a playground for the theatrics of male chauvinists. As Etoke (2006:41) has pointed out: "Female figures mainly operate as abstract bodies [...] The woman's body becomes the battleground of conflicting discourses on nationalism, identity and sexuality." Africa is filled with cultural practices that legitimate the notion of a docile female body.

The practice of virginity testing where the absence of a small tissue becomes a big issue is a case in point. Every year in South Africa, for example, thousands of Zulu maidens participate in the *Umhlanga*[12], celebrating virginity. Tens of thousands of teenagers, wearing nothing but strings of beads and colorful loincloth submit themselves to the ordeal of having a stranger stick a finger in their private parts to check if their hymens are intact. They leap for joy when the tests confirm that they are virgins. The young girls undergoing genital examination to determine their virginity lay on a grass mat while the operation is taking place. The tester, usually an elderly woman, uses a single pair of gloves while examining the teenagers. Sometimes it is carried out with bare hands and the tester seldom washes her hands! Girls who pass the test have white stars pasted on their foreheads and a certificate confirming their virginity is given to them. If a girl passes the test, the women ululate and clap their hands but when she fails, an accusing silence follows her; she is asked to sit in a corner and wait for an older woman who comes to counsel her. Girls who fail the test are usually shunned and subjected to psychological and emotional trauma. Virginity testing thus becomes an ordeal for these young girls.

Despite the notoriety of this practice throughout Africa, critics view it as a violation of the right of the girl child. They argue that the practice is unconstitutional and violates the human rights of those being tested. Others argue that the practice violates children's right to privacy, bodily integrity and dignity. This writer contends that virginity testing undermines the principles of equality, freedom and human dignity. According to an article published by the United Nations (UN) Office for the Coordination of Humanitarian Affairs (2007:2), the South African Commission on Gender Equality has described virginity testing as "discriminatory, invasive of privacy, unfair, impinging on the dignity of young girls and unconstitutional." This notwithstanding, proponents argue that the practice is the best way to curb sexual promiscuity, unwanted teenage pregnancy and the spread of HIV/AIDS.

Persuasive as these arguments may be, the fact of the matter is that only scant attention is being paid to the health hazards and the emotional burden put on young girls undergoing virginity testing. Social workers in South Africa and other parts of Africa have noted that pressure emanating from virginity testing is resulting in young girls engaging in anal and oral intercourse in order to keep their status as virgins intact. Jambaya (2007:2) points out that if a girl is found to have had sex she is "open to being ostracized by the community and subjected to all forms of abuse." The questions that beg asking are: What about boys? Why aren't they being tested? Are boys not sexually promiscuous? I believe that boys and girls should be given equal treatment. The boy child should be taught moral rectitude as well, if this is the ultimate goal of virginity testing. By putting the onus of sexual responsibility only on girls, this writer contends that virginity testing is sexist. It is discriminatory. This sort of unfair discrimination stigmatizes the female gender by creating the false impression that women are inherently erratic in their comportment.

Worse still, virginity testing may contribute to the spread of HIV/AIDS given the widely held belief in some parts of Africa that having unprotected sex with a virgin may serve as a cure for AIDS. Girls who pass the test may be targeted by male predators. Another negative aspect of virginity testing is that it relies on shame and fear rather than free choice, to dissuade teenagers from engaging in pre-marital sex. It also overlooks cases where the hymen of a girl may be ruptured as a result of engaging in physically exacting activities such as sports. Moreover, these tests fail to take into account involuntary sexual encounters such as rape. A girl who has been raped would undergo trauma on several levels if she had to undergo a virginity test.

On this count, many girls, out of shame, are reluctant to report that they have been raped. For these reasons, it may be argued that we are fighting a losing battle given that the whole exercise is not foolproof. These are some of the intriguing issues that advocates of virginity testing have not been able to address. To make matters worse, the practice has now been made to serve utilitarian purposes: parents want their daughters to undergo virginity testing in the most part because their daughters would fetch them a higher *lobola*[13] if they passed the test.

Virginity testing is not the only abuse the African woman has to deal with. In her novel *C'est le soleil qui m'a brûlé* (1987), Cameroonian feminist writer Calixthe Beyala underscores the traumatic experience of rape on women. She shows how rape has become emblematic of the sexual tensions existing between men and women in Africa. The novel highlights the fate of Ateba, a young woman whose life in the slums of Cameroon vacillates between poverty, solitude and sexual violence. According to Baumeister and Tice (2001:163), "Rape is about power and domination." In other words, it is a power struggle in which men attempt to impose their views on women. A reading of Beyala's novel reveals a feeling of rebellion and a yearning for liberation on the part of the rape victim: "*La tête dans les odeurs de l'homme, la bouche contre son sexe [...] Et si elle arrêtait le cours de l'histoire en arrachant son sexe à coup de dents?* » [Her head in the man's odors, her mouth against his genitalia [...] What if she could stop the course of history by cutting his sex with her teeth?]. Thus rape destabilizes our society by creating an atmosphere of animosity between males and females.

Another cultural practice that puts the life of African women in jeopardy is female genital mutilation. (FGM) This practice has been christened the scourge of Africa by global feminists. Abusharaf (2006:5) has drawn attention to the joint statement issued in April 1997 by W.H.O, UNICEF and UNFPA that defines female genital mutilation as "All procedures involving partial or total removal of the external genitalia or other injury to the female genital organs whether for cultural or other non-therapeutic reasons." Female genital mutilation is most prevalent in African countries such as Nigeria, Ethiopia, Sudan, Niger, Somalia, Chad and Egypt. It is not restricted to any ethnic, religious or socioeconomic class. Many reasons account for the perpetuation of this practice, the most common being cultural and religious beliefs. Interestingly enough, some African women believe that FGM makes them more feminine and thus more attractive to men! Some African men argue that FGM raises the social status of the family and generates income when the daughter gets married and the dowry is paid. Like virginity testing, therefore, this age-old practice has been made to serve pecuniary ends because a premium is placed on its financial benefits.

Female genital mutilation is traditionally performed by elderly women who have no medical skills at all. According to Hamilton (1997:1), "They use unsterilized razor blades, kitchen implements, or even broken glass." In the short term, mutilated girls and women may experience severe pain, shock, urine retention, ulceration of the genital region, or even fatal hemorrhage. Long-term adverse effects of FGM include cysts and abscesses, keloid scarring, urinary incontinence, dyspareunia, sexual dysfunction, urinary tract infection, infertility and complications during childbirth. Faced with a problem of this magnitude, the heads of the World Health Organization (W.H.O), UNICEF and the United Nations Population Fund have called for an end to what they see as an unsafe and unjustifiable cultural practice. Margaret Brady (1999:1) has noted that "various degrees of FGM are prevalent, the most mutilating one being infibulation." With infibulation there are numerous life-long health hazards such as hemorrhage, infection, genital ulcers, and gynecological and obstetrical complications. It has also been postulated that FGM plays a significant role in facilitating the transmission of HIV infection through numerous mechanisms.

In her novel, *La petite peule* (2000), Guinean writer Mariama Barry brings the issue of female genital mutilation to the forefront. According to Etoke (op cit, 41), Barry "reveals how the woman's body works as a mediator that finds a compromise between a need for freedom and socio-cultural mechanisms that regulate the life of the individual." Etoke points out that in this compelling narrative about female genital mutilation, we find that Barry's writing portrays the suffering female body as suffocated because of her inability to escape from traditional ways of thinking which repress any display of emotion. Barry (op cit, 13) describes the painful experience of the mutilated girl as follows:

> Je perçus entre mes jambes le contact glacial de quelque chose de tranchant. Sur le coup je n'ai pas réalisé la douleur, je ne voulais plus penser à mon mal. [I felt a cold contact between my legs, something sharp. At the moment I did not realize the pain. I did not want to think about my pain anymore.]

The novelist deliberately refrains from naming the object used in mutilating the woman's body. Rather she puts emphasis on the victim's feigned stoicism— the attempt to resist and to forget her ordeal. Etoke notes (op cit, 42):

> Barry negotiates a literary space in which it is possible to tell a traumatizing individual experience when you belong to a society where female sexual mutilation is first and foremost understood as a cultural practice that helps in maintaining traditional values and social cohesion.

Kourouma (1970:31-32) views female genital mutilation differently. In his novel *Les soleils des indépendances* he depicts it as rape:

> *Le viol! Dans le sang et les douleurs de l'excision, elle a été mordue par les feux du fer chauffé au rouge et du piment. Et elle a crié, hurlé. Et ses yeux ont tourné, débordé et plongé dans le vert de la forêt puis le jaune de l'harmattan et enfin le rouge, le rouge du sang, le rouge des sacrifices. Et elle a encore hurlé, crié à tout chauffer, crié de toute sa poitrine, crié jusqu'à s'étouffer, jusqu'à perdre connaissance.*
>
> [Rape! Amidst the blood and pain of excision, something had seared her like fiery pepper, like red-hot-iron. She had screamed, howled. Her eyes had spun round, spilled over and plunged into the green of forest, the yellow of the harmattan wind, then red, blood-red, the red of sacrifice. And she had screamed again, screamed as loudly as possible, with all her strength; screamed until she choked and fainted.][14]

Thus, in contradistinction to Barry who perceives female genital mutilation as a rite of passage, Kourouma decries its harmful effects. According to Abusharaf(op cit,1), "*Bolokobi, khifad, tahara, tahoor, qodiin, irua, bondo, kuruna, negekorigin, and kene-kene* are some of the terms employed in African indigenous languages to denote a set of cultural practices collectively known as female circumcision." Most of these terms could be translated as ritual purification or rite of passage.

The World Health Organization (1994:22) estimates that "over 130 million girls and women have undergone genital excision and at least two million per year are expected to go through the practice." Health authorities in Italy estimated that 40,000 women of African origin, mostly Somalis, have undergone the practice and 5000 young girls are currently at risk. The Centers for Disease Control and Prevention estimated that, in the United States of America alone, more than 150,000 women and girls of African origin have already been cut or might have the operation performed on them (Hundley 2002).

Abusharaf (op cit, 4) further observes that "Numerous groups in Africa are grappling with these practices, which have proven harmful to women and girls, in an attempt to end them once and for all."

Feminist discourse around the world underscores the fact that female genital mutilation is a form of violence against women, indistinguishable from rape, human trafficking, physical and emotional abuse, and sexual harassment. They have portrayed the practice as a symptom of female victimization by a patriarchal society keen on controlling women's sexuality (Eisler, 1995; Hicks, 1996; Hosken, 1994; Lightfoot-Klein, 2003; Okin, 1999; Walker and Parmar, 1993). Some gender activists argue that the practice infringes upon human rights conventions intended to protect and defend women from violence and aggression, notably the UN Declaration on Violence against Women (1993) and the UN High Commission on Refugee Statement Against Gender-Based Violence (1996). This writer sees female circumcision as a form of castration that deprives the woman of sexual pleasure and in so doing violates her right to corporeal and sexual integrity. Zwang (1997:1) may be right when he points out that "Ablation of the clitoris during infancy prevents the establishment of the reflex circuit, and the woman will never be able to experience clitoral or vaginal pleasure."

The woman's right to corporeal integrity is equally violated through the age-old custom that allows widow inheritance in Africa. Wife inheritance is widely practised among ethnic groups in Kenya, Uganda, Tanzania, the Democratic Republic of the Congo, Sudan and Cameroon, to name but a few. Most men who inherit widows have multiple sex partners because they have inherited other widows. Ignorance and unwillingness to wear condoms often lead to the spread of HIV in such polygamous families. A study carried out by Okeyo (1994:1) shows that "sexual intercourse is an essential component of widow inheritance." In other words, men's uncontrollable libido leads them into marrying the widows of deceased relatives. Okeyo notes that, the eldest son of a polygamous husband who dies leaving behind young wives is entitled to "inherit" the youngest stepmother. To justify this practice, wife inheritors call it "widow guardianship".

In her novel *So Long a Letter* (1980:57), Senegalese writer Mariama Bâ addresses the question of widow inheritance. The novel recounts in epistolary form the story of a Senegalese woman, Ramatoulaye, whose husband dies after many years of polygamous marriage. His brother, Tamsir, uses tradition and religion (Islam) as a justification to marry his late brother's wife:

> When you have come out (that is to say, of mourning), I shall marry you. You suit me as a wife, and further, you will continue to live here, just as if Modou were not dead. Usually, it is the younger brother who inherits his elder brother's wife. In this case, it is the opposite. You are my good luck. I shall marry you.

By bringing the oddity of this practice under the spotlight, Bâ, I believe, speaks for all the oppressed women in Africa and beyond. As she has pointed out in her non-fictional work (1981:7), "It is up to us women to take our fate in our hands in order to overthrow the order established to our detriment instead of submitting to it." In the aforementioned novel she illustrates that Senegalese society functions as though all wives come from a lower class than their husbands. Although only the specific offense of Tamsir's action is named here, the larger wrong is that society allows such practices to take place. As Klaw (2000:136) has noted, "Ramatoulaye's narrative deconstructs several of the essential definitions that the dominant order uses to justify its actions." Bâ's protagonist raises her voice in protest against patriarchal tyranny by refusing categorically to marry her late husband's brother:

> My voice has known silence for thirty years; thirty years of harassment [...] You forget that I have a heart, a mind that I am not an object to be passed from hand to hand. You don't know what marriage means to me: it is an act of faith and of love, the total surrender of oneself to the person one has chosen and who has chosen you. (58)

These words of dissidence call into question a tradition that has gone unquestioned for generations. By questioning the raison d'être of arranged or forced marriages, Bâ is appealing for a change in Senegalese mentality. Riesz (1991:27) notes that "critics have generally regarded Mariama *Bâ's Une si long lettre* as a novel about marriage, about how and why [...] marriages failed in a Senegalese Islamic context." I believe that the failure of marriages in such African societies is attributable to the fact they are contracted for the wrong reasons. For example, Binetou"s marriage to Modou in *So Long a Letter* illustrates blind devotion to traditional materialism. She feels caught in a double blind when she agrees to marry Modou. She does not wish to suffer for the rest of her life married to an old man; but at the same time, she does not want her mother to hate her for not giving her a rich and easy old age: "Her mother cried so much. She begged her daughter to give her a happy ending in a real house that the man promised them. So she agreed." (55) Bâ pointedly remarks: "Sold, she raised her price each day."(72) The theme of Bâ's novel, I believe, is gender equality. As she has pointed out: "I remain convinced of the obligatory, inescapable complementarity of man and woman."(129) She thinks that freedom of choice in marriage would result in harmonious co-existence in the community and probably put an end to gender oppression in Africa.

Gender inequality accounts for the rampant practice of arranged marriages on the continent. In traditional African societies girls are given in marriage in their teens in order to ensure obedience and subservience to their husbands. In Ethiopia and parts of West Africa, for example, marriage before the age of fourteen is common. In Kebbi State in Northern Nigeria, the average age of marriage for girls is just over 11, against a national average of 17. Strange as it may sound, it is true that some African communities persist in perceiving the girl child as an object to toy with. Indigent families often regard their daughters as economic assets. In North Africa, for instance, girls as young as ten are being sent off to marriage in order for the parents to reap financial benefits. To put this in another way, growing poverty in Africa has put young girls at risk of forced marriages. Parents who can no longer fend for themselves opt to trade off their children for money. When this happens, the girl becomes "owned" and feels powerless in the matrimonial home. In villages throughout northern Malawi, girls are often married at or before puberty to whomever their fathers choose, sometimes to husbands as much as a quarter century older. Worse still, at times, the girls are asked to abandon school and become wives.

More often than not, these girls have no one to turn to when complications arise in the matrimonial homes. Those who are not subservient are often subjected to battery by their husbands. In Egypt, studies show that 29% of young brides have been beaten by their husbands or relatives. Domestic violence often causes girls to run away, and in several countries this can trigger "honor killings" by male relatives eager to wipe out a perceived smear on the family. It should be noted that the practice of forcing girls into marriage started centuries ago throughout Sub-Saharan Africa but it continues to be widespread, especially in countries with large Muslim communities. Monekosso (2001:3) has observed that, "Teenage marriages are also common in conflict situations ..." where girls have been made to serve as "wives" in military zones.

It is interesting to note that early marriages are closely linked to repeated and unplanned childbearing. UNICEF stresses the fact that child marriages inflict tremendous physical and emotional hardship on young women all over the world. Death rates are also high because teenage bodies are not ready for the rigors of pregnancy and childbirth yet. Pregnancy-related deaths are the leading cause of mortality for child mothers. Medical professionals have pointed out that pre-adolescent marriage is partly responsible for Africa's high maternal mortality rates, one of the highest in the world. In sum, the consequences of forced marriages are many: early pregnancies, hazardous births, school dropout, and unemployment among others. The list has grown to include HIV at an age when girls do not fully understand the risks involved in uncontrolled sexual conduct.

This writer maintains that teenage marriages could be brought to an end by educating young girls and their parents on the health hazards and other mishaps associated with the practice. Another way to address the issue would be to organize national campaigns to raise awareness on this problem. Child marriage is a tradition that tends to be passed down through generations because parents were brought up in the same manner. Worse still, most parents are not aware of the dangers involved, or might even feel that the dangers are justified for cultural reasons. Even when parents and children understand the negative implications of teenage marriages, pressure exerted by society on families to conform may be great. Be it as it may, these attitudes have to change in order for our society to make progress. Customs promoting adolescent marriages need to be challenged. The media (TV, radio and newspapers) could play a significant role in calling attention to attitudes and customs that encourage child marriages. Incentives meant to encourage parents to send their female children to school would also be valuable.

Cameroonian playwright Guillaume Oyono Mbia has fictionalized the problem of forced marriages in his play titled *Three Suitors: One Husband* (1968) set in the village of Mvoutessi, in the southern part of East Cameroon. In this play, Juliette, a daughter from the village, returns home from secondary school with Oko, her fiancé, whom she intends to introduce to her family. But other arrangements for her marriage had already been made by her father, Atangana Abessolo, and all her relatives expect her to comply. Mosadomi (2000:1) describes this culturally rich play as an "epigraphic comment on love, marriage, tradition and personal pursuit of happiness." Mbia's play portrays an individual crisis in the sense that the protagonist finds it hard to understand why an educated girl like her should have a husband imposed on her. At the same time, the play is a collective crisis in that Juliette's marriage is only one of many such marriages being negotiated behind the backs of girls in her community. She is astonished at this transaction that transforms her into a commodity and a source of wealth for her father and the community at large. Her bewilderment is voiced when she screams:

> What? Am I for sale? Are you trying to give me to the highest bidder? Why can't you ask me my opinion about my own marriage? [...] So you are expecting me to make you rich! Am I a shop, or some other source of income? (15-16)

In a male-dominated society like Mvoutessi this reaction is unacceptable. That is why her outraged father expresses his shock:

> Since when do women speak in Mvoutessi? Who teaches you girls of today such disgraceful behavior? Why are you always trying to have a say in every matter? (15)

The reaction of Juliette's father lends credibility to the claim that in traditional Africa men expect women to be seen and not heard. In many African communities, marriage is considered consummated only after *lobola* (bride price) has been paid. The payment of bride price is widespread and entrenched in Africa. It is a custom that requires a man to give money and possibly goods such as livestock to his would-be wife's family. In South Africa, for instance, *lobola* may amount to several head of cattle. These days some families ask for payment in cash. According to Derby (2006:1), "The tradition of *lobola*, or dowry, has long been common throughout southern Africa as the groom's family gives a gift, typically cattle, to the family whose daughter is joining their household." In its most benign form, *lobola* is a token of appreciation from the groom's family to the bride's. At its most egregious, it turns girls into the human equivalent of cattle.

Women rights activists are working hard to abolish *lobola* because it creates a financial incentive for parents to marry off their daughters sooner rather than later. In most communities, bride price negotiations are typically male discussions of down payments, installments, settlements and the occasional refund of dowry for a wife who runs away. In the event of divorce, the bride's family is required to pay back the *lobola*. In some countries such as Uganda, men demand a full refund of the bride price if a marriage breaks up. This effectively prevents women from leaving abusive matrimonial homes given that repayment of lobola places a huge financial burden on some families. The payment of bride price has wide-ranging implications for the bride's freedom or absence thereof. Although the practice was conceived as a token of gratitude to the parents of the bride for raising the woman one fell in love with, this practice has been appropriated and turned into a business transaction by opportunistic people. Derby notes that several years ago, a Johannesburg businessman was asked to pay $250,000 for the hand of the daughter of Zulu King Goodwill Zwelithini. Little wonder that after paying such astronomical sums of money some men go away with the impression that they have "bought" their wives. By the same token, the husband starts to regard his wife as his "property". In other words, some men soon begin to develop a false sense of ownership of their spouses. This explains why wife battery and rape often go unreported.

Domestic violence is, indeed, a thorny problem in most parts of Africa where women are savaged by their husbands with flimsy excuses. This is because most men have a false sense of entitlement which, surprisingly, is sometimes expressed in the man's claim to the right to keep mistresses. In the Republic of Cameroon, for example, most men have *deuxième bureaux*[15]. The solution to this spousal abuse, I believe, resides in the education and economic empowerment of the African woman. Education would raise awareness among women not only to the deleterious effects of gender oppression but also to a new form of female abuse that has surfaced in many parts of Africa: breast ironing.

A nationwide campaign is underway in Cameroon to discourage the widespread practice of breast-ironing. Breast-ironing is a form of body modification where mothers, aunts and older female members of the family flatten the breast of pubescent girls in an attempt to make them less sexually attractive to men. According to Sa'ah (2006:1) "Breast ironing involves pounding and massaging the developing breasts of young girls with hot objects to try to make them disappear." The most common instruments used to flatten the breasts of young girls in Cameroon and other African countries are wooden pestles, used for pounding tubers in the kitchen. Heated bananas, coconut shells and grinding stones are also used. Interviewed by Sa'ah (op cit, 1), Geraldin Sirri, a Cameroonian student, recounts her ordeal:

> My mother took a pestle, she warmed it well in the fire and then she used it to pound my breasts while I was lying down. She took the back of a coconut, warmed in the fire and used it to iron my breasts. I was crying and trembling to escape but there was no way.

Strangely enough, some girls iron their own breasts in the mistaken belief that doing so would help them escape from early marriage. Vaiza (2006:10) has pointed out that "the practice is carried out in almost every nation of Africa, mainly in the regions of Chad, Togo, Benin, Guinea-Conakry and Cameroon." Girls as young as twelve years old are subjected to this humiliating custom. No matter how painful and barbarous the practice may be, girls are afraid of defying what they see as a ritual or rite of passage. Nonetheless, women rights activists are leaving no stone unturned to eradicate this nefarious cultural practice.

Cameroonian parents who iron the breasts of their daughters do so because they believe that when a girl has breasts, she attracts male attention, have sex, and become pregnant. Ironically, breast-ironing is not an effective method of preventing early sex and unwanted pregnancies because many of the teenage girls who have had their breasts flattened still fall pregnant. The solution to this problem, I think, is education. It is incumbent upon parents to educate their children on the hazards of premature sexual intercourse. They should school their children on the basics of sexual reproductive health so they are aware of what it means growing up and having breasts or having menstrual periods.

Breast-ironing, it seems to me, is as bad as female genital mutilation and virginity testing because it is one of those misogynistic contraptions conceived by men to manipulate female bodies. The effects are devastating and traumatizing. Massaging the breasts of young girls is very dangerous and harmful to health. Health care professionals have pointed out the dangers associated with breast-ironing. They point out that the emotional scars associated with the practice are overwhelming. Some social workers wonder how a girl can ever get over the fact that her parents, the people she trusted the most in her life, destroyed her breasts so that she wouldn't have sex. These stories leave one with the feeling that some of our customs ought to be questioned and challenged because they are counterproductive. Our women need proper education in order to play an effective role in the fight against gender oppression.

Speaking to 'Africa Today' Senegalese musical virtuoso, Baaba Maa (2005:38) points out:

> Majority of African women are uneducated, unemployed and have limited opportunities in trade or government […] In the lyrics of my song I talked about an African woman one day joining the good male leaders to lead the continent out of our predicament because women have the power and have shown the determination when they get the opportunity.

Women play a crucial role in nation-building the world over. Africa is no exception. If we continue to put our womenfolk on the back burner our continent will stagnate in perpetuity because the development of the African continent requires collective effort. There is no gainsaying the fact that African women are as capable as their men. Liberian Head of State, Ellen Johnson Sirleaf has made history by being elected the first female president on the African continent! Kenyan university don Wangari Maathai has done Africa proud by winning the prestigious Nobel Prize for her sterling achievement in the field of environmentalism! Africans need to discard age-old customs that are keeping us in the dark. We must place men and women on an equal footing in all walks of life. There are no inherently inferior sexes.

As French feminist writer Simone de Beauvoir has argued in her book *Le deuxième sexe* (1949:13) gender is a social construct:

> *On ne naît pas femme: on le devient. Aucun destin biologique, psychique, économique ne définit la figure que revêt au sein de la société la femelle humaine; c'est l'ensemble de la civilisation qui élabore ce produit intermédiaire entre le mâle et le castrat qu'on qualifie de féminin.*

> [One is not born, but rather becomes a woman. No biological, pschological, or economic fate determines the figure that the human female presents in society; it is civilization as a whole that produces this creature, intermediate between male and eunuch, which is described as feminine.][16]

Thus Beauvoir underscores the role played by prejudice in the oppression of women in contemporary societies. She points out that the key to understanding how girls develop as opposed to boys is to be found not in any "myth of the second sex" but in the manner of their upbringing in a society geared toward male supremacy. In other words, women consider themselves inferior because men regard them as such. Beauvoir offers her views on the subtle ways in which matrimony has often been made to work to the detriment of women. She perceives marriage as a male contraption to perpetuate gender inequality when she notes:

> *Le mariage s'est toujours présenté de manière radicalement différente pour l'homme et pour la femme. Les deux sexes sont nécessaires l'un à l'autre, mais cette nécessité n'a jamais engendré entre eux de réciprocité ; jamais les femmes n'ont constitué une caste établissant avec la caste mâle sur un pied d'égalité des échanges et des contrats. Socialement l'homme est un individu autonome et complet [...] On a vu pour quelles raisons le rôle reproducteur et domestique dans lequel*

*est cantonnée la femme ne lui a pas garanti une égale dignité.
(196)*

[Mariage has always been a very different thing for man and for woman. The two sexes are necessary to each other, but this necessity has never brought about a condition of reciprocity between them; women, as we have seen, have never constituted a caste making exchanges and contracts with the male caste upon a footing of equality. A man is socially an independent and complete individual [...] We have seen why it is that the reproductive and domestic role to which woman is confined has not guaranteed her an equal dignity.][17]

I argue along with Beauvoir and others that the second-class status to which the African woman has been confined is a social construct. I further contend that gender discourse in Africa needs to be revisited and re-orientated to address issues that center on gender inequality. Finally, I posit that the African woman is in dire need of proper education in order to fight male oppression. It is my conviction that a woman's consciousness of her own femininity is to be defined under circumstances dependent on the society of which she is a member. Indeed, a major thesis of this discussion is that all her life the African woman is to find the magic of her mirror a tremendous help in her effort to project herself in order to attain self-liberation. It is in the context of their natural differences that African men and women must assert their commonality.

Chapter Seven
AFRICAN TIME AND OTHER AFRICANISMS

It boggles the mind to think that in this day and time, some Africans continue to uphold the antiquated notion of 'African time'. All too often, one finds people of color walking leisurely into boardroom at 2:00pm to attend a meeting that was scheduled for 12:00pm. The flimsy excuse often advanced to justify this collective misconduct is the irksome misnomer called "African time" which could be translated as "no time". As far as the logic of "African time" goes, breakfast could be eaten at lunch time; lunch at dinner time and vice versa. This sort of backwoods mentality belongs in the past. It stems from a primitive mindset which restricts Africans to reading time by observing their own shadows, movements of the sun and moon or listening to the crow of the cock. Such reasoning also confines Africans to counting rivers, streams, mountains and hills in order to measure distances between villages and towns. This is a load of hogwash! This is the twenty-first century. We cannot continue to submit ourselves to this kind of *"before for back"*[18] mentality.

Decency and good breeding dictate that people should be punctual at all times. Being on time shows that we respect others. Punctuality, I believe, is a mark of self-discipline and respect toward others. We cannot continue to behave like a bunch of unruly school kids all in the name of "African time". Time plays a crucial role in every walk of life. In the corporate world, time is money. All workers are paid on the basis of time computation. In academia time management distinguishes underachievers from overachievers. Time has become an overbearing master in our lives. The concept of time is of such critical importance that communication pundits have coined the term 'chronemics' *to* describe the use of time in interpersonal communication. This writer attaches so much importance to time that he has written an entire poem in honor of time:

TIME'S MONEY

Time is pregnant with meaning:
Time and tide wait for no one,
A stitch in time saves nine,
Procrastination is the thief of time.

There's time for everything:

Time to be born;
And time to die.
Time to jubilate;
And time to lament.
Time to work;
And time to rest.
Time to sow;
And time to harvest.
Time to procrastinate;
And time to act.

In bread-and-butter world,
Time is money,
Modus operandi for bread-winning,
Humanity and time are locked
in a vicious circle devoid of exit.

Folks can't eat anymore!
Folks can't rest anymore!
*Man no rest, day de go
mandat de bole!*[19]
Folks can't play anymore!
All play and no work,
Makes Tara a *mbut*.[20]
Folks can't commune anymore!
Time's become an over-bearing master!

Homes are ripped asunder,
Parents vie with one another
for mundane wealth.
Children left to their own devices have
the leeway to do to their heart's content.
I wonder if this infernal
race will ever come to an end.[21]

    Another obtrusive behavior that seems endemic to Africa is that of loud-speaking. Someone once joked that if you met a group of people in the street talking as if they were about to start throwing punches at one another they are most likely to be Africans. Another person jested that Africans talk the way they do because having been bedfellows with monkeys, chimpanzees and baboons for a very long time; they have internalized the manner in which their simian cousins chatter. Offensive as these jokes may seem, each one harbors an iota of truth.

In sum, as we celebrate our African heritage we should be mindful of the fact that some of our mannerisms are keeping us in the dark. "African time", "loquaciousness", and "loud-speaking" are some of these attitudes.

Chapter Eight
MANUFACTURING THE ILLUSION OF FREEDOM

As the winds of change continue to blow over Africa, the continent's intelligentsia and friends of Africa spend sleepless nights brainstorming on possible remedies that may cure the myriad maladies afflicting the continent. Africa's most contagious ailment at present, it seems to me, it that of misgovernment. Africa continues to be poorly governed by a bunch of greedy self-seekers "who have invented neither powder nor compass", to borrow the expression of the celebrated Caribbean poet and playwright, Aimé Césaire (1983:95). This class of comprador bourgeoisie[22] is good for nothing but "apemanship" and "parrotology" to borrow the phrase of another illustrious son of Africa, Ngugi wa Thiong'o. Thinkers such as Frantz Fanon (1968) have emphasized the fact that the Third World bourgeoisie are far different from their Western counterparts in that they have not risen to power through the historical process of Cultural Revolution but have merely been placed in power by their former colonial masters. As a result, according to Fanon, this bourgeoisie lacks the historical energy and vitality of its Western predecessors, of whom it is merely a weak and prematurely decadent echo.

The struggle to decolonize Africa economically and extricate her from the grip of Western imperialistic vultures is a task too important to be left in the hands of intellectual Lilliputians.[23] Meaningful development in Africa requires commitment by Africans from all walks of life. Above all, African leaders must rid themselves of what Franz Fanon (1967:115) has termed the "mentality of the colonized" in his classic work *Black Skin White Masks*.

This presupposes casting off the colonial mindset characterized by a culture of subservience. Most African presidents still comport themselves like elementary school pupils suffering from compulsive paranoia. The case of President Paul Biya of the Republic of Cameroon who once declared himself the "meilleur élève du Président François Mitterrand"[24] of France is a case in point. It is significant in this context to point out that the assimilationist policies of France had an enormous impact on the way French-speaking Africans view themselves, especially in their relation with the metropole. Mr. Biya presents us with an example of the insecurities of Francophone African politicians who take their cues from Paris rather than from their own people. After his marriage to Chantal Vigoroux on 23rd April 1994 following the death of former first lady Jeanne Irene Atyam, this lame duck president has been behaving as if he is out of his mind. Chantal has virtually hypnotized him and made herself the de facto vice-president of Cameroon, calling the shots left, right and center. Smith (2006:1) may be right when she describes Biya's marriage to this métis[25] born in Yaoundé to a Lebanese father and Cameroonian mother as the "worst blunder or marriage of an African leader to a second wife." Smith points out that Chantal Biya has a well furnished bank account at the French Bank BNP, the Bank of African dictators, thier wives and entourage. She also has a well supplied account with another French bank, Credit Lyonnais. This bank is where the petroleum monies of Cameroon have been deposited by Mr. Biya. Kourouma (1990:266) satirizes the deplorable conduct of African leaders when he writes:

> *Ceux de Soba comme tous les Africains plus tard vivront l'ère des présidents fondateurs des partis uniques, dont certains décréteront que tous les habitants du pays sont members du parti et préléveront comme la capitation des*
>
> *cotisations qu'ils feront encaisser sans attribuer ni carte ni acquit. Avec les fonds jamais comptabilisés ou contrôlés, ou nom du combat sacré pour l'unité nationale, de la lutte contre l'impérialisme, le sous-développement et la famine, ils se construiront des villas de rapport, entretiendront de nombreuses maîtresses, planqueront de l'argent en Suisse et achèteront en Europe des châteaux où ils se réfugieront après les immanquables putschs qui les chasseront du pouvoir.*

[The people of Soba, like all Africans, would experience the era of one-party systems and founding presidents, some of whom will decree that everyone in the country was a party member, will collect membership dues as if they were a per capita tax and they'll pocket the money without giving any card or receipt. With these funds that are never verified or accounted for in the name of the sacred cause of national unity, the struggle against imperialism, underdevelopment and famine, they'll build themselves income-producing houses, they will keep numrerous mistresses, stash money Switzerland and buy châteaux in Europe where they'll take refuge after the inevitable putsch that will chase them from power.]

Here Kourouma makes a direct attack on African political leaders and the manner in which they govern their nations as if they were passersby. The diatribe is quite blunt. There is a sense of appeal to the governed to come to terms with leaders who continue to betray them on political and economic fronts.

President Biya is a typical example of such African political leaders. He has made himself an absentee tenant of Etoudi[26]. He frequently takes off to France and other European countries where he spends months. Cameroonians are dumbfounded by the head of state's misconduct. Rebel novelist Mongo Beti (1980:120) has castigated Mr. Biya's dereliction of duty in one of his novels *Trop de soleil tue l'amour* as follows:

> *Quand le grand chef disparaît de chez nous là pour passer deux mois à Baden-Baden là, tu vas même lui dire que quoi? Je te demande, Norbert, qui va même lui dire que quoi?*
> [When the big boss disappears from the country to spend two months in Baden-Baden, what do you have to tell him? I am asking you, Norbert, who can say what to him?]

Like Chantal Biya, Grace Mugabe, the second wife of the dictatorial president of Zimbabwe, is calling the shots in Harare. Grace is virtually the vice-president of Zimbabwe. It is my conviction that it would take a popular uprising, in fact, a revolution to get rid of these political leeches in Africa. By their very nature revolutions are led by the downtrodden, the wretched of the earth, people who have nothing to lose. To paraphrase the central thesis in Fanon's *The Wretched of the Earth* (1963), only through a violent political revolution can Africans rid themselves of a slave mentality that accepts social inequalities. In Decolonizing *the Mind* (1986:80) Ngugi wa Thiong'o wonders aloud with regard to the slave mentality of African leaders:

> How does a writer, a novelist, shock his readers by telling them that these [heads of state who collaborate with imperial powers] are neo-slaves when they themselves, the neo-slaves, are openly announcing the fact on the rooftops? How do you shock your readers by pointing out that these are mass murderers, looters, robbers, thieves, when they, the perpetrators of these anti-people crimes, are not even attempting to hide the fact? When in some cases they are actually and proudly celebrating their massacre of children, and the theft and robbery of the nation? How do you satirize their utterances and claims when their own words beat all fictional exaggerations?

The success of a revolution is determined by the degree of commitment of the people determined to bring about meaningful change. Arguing along the same lines, Rial (1972:12) contends that the total liberation of Africa will be achieved via two revolutions. As he sees it, Africans have successfully carried out one revolution, political independence. The second, socio-economic, is still to come:

> L'Afrique ne sera vraiment libre qu'après une double
> révolution. La première politique, a eu lieu. Elle a
> donné l'indépendance aux Africains. La seconde,
> sociale, reste à faire.
> [Africa shall really be free only after a two-fold
> revolution. The first, political independence, has
> been achieved; the second, social, is yet to come.

The struggle to liberate Africa from inept leadership calls for the involvement of Africa's intelligentsia at home and in the Diaspora. We have to desist from paying lip service to our liberation struggle. We've got to call a spade a spade. The plain truth is that Africa has gained independence but not yet its freedom. African countries have achieved political independence providing them with a new sense of responsibility, and yet a foreign presence continues to haunt them. If it means dismantling existing political systems in order to re-construct, so be it! Like my friends in Swine Quarter in Bamenda would have it, "*man no die, man no rotten!*"[27] It makes no sense to stand hands akimbo gazing into the sky while one's home is ablaze.

In the struggle to free Africa from neo-colonial yoke, the genuine African intellectual must be distinguished from the armchair critic who is neither a man of action nor a change agent. As Madamombe (2007:17) has pointed out:

> The role of our intellectuals should be to
> enhance the capacity of the continent to mobilize
> the vast human capital and natural wealth in
> order to eradicate the endemic poverty and
> stagnation that have become our lot for so long.

Arguing along similar lines, Yoder (1991:177) has pointed out that "[...] the destiny of Africa is closely related to the personal success and moral integrity of its elite."

In this essay, I have argued that the onus is on all Africans, regardless of gender, age-group, ethnic origin or creed, to take up the cudgels and do battle with the forces of evil and destabilization in order to put Africa back on the rails of development. The time for spectatorship is over! As Césaire (1968:22) has cautioned, life is not a spectacle:

> [...] *Gardez-vous de vous croiser les bras en l'attitude stérile du spectateur, car la vie n'est pas un spectacle, car une mer de douleurs n'est pas un proscenium, car un homme qui crie n'est pas un ours qui danse..."*
>
> [And most of all beware, even in the thought of assuming the sterile attitude of the spectator, for life is not a spectacle, a sea of grief is not a proscenium, and a man who wails is not a dancing bear...]

Put differently, Africans will act or perish. It has now become a do-or-die battle. We cannot continue to play romance with our enemies. It is incumbent upon us all to work in tandem for genuine freedom in Africa. We are not yet free! Let's not lie to ourselves. Africans have to make sure that their continent is free politically and economically. They have to do everything possible to halt civil strife on the continent. Civil wars constitute an obstacle to the development of Africa. As Kambudzi (op cit, 8) has observed, "Civil wars are more recurrent and tend to embrace more than one state on the continent." Given the weak nature of African economies, civil wars tend to be disruptive because it is costly to restore economic vitality after a war.

Chapter Nine
MYTH ABOUT AFRICA'S COLLECTIVE AMNESIA

It is hard to disagree with a weighty viewpoint expressed by a concerned Africanist. In an article titled 'Away with double standards' published in the July edition of *Africa Today* Emmanuel Yartney (2004:2) contends:

> The developed nations of Europe and the United States are responsible for the acute hunger in the developing world because of their unnecessary interference in the governance of less powerful countries.

For centuries, Western powers have systematically destabilized Africa and siphoned her wealth through covert activities ranging from their roles in genocides, civil wars, the looting of mineral and land resources, and the overthrow of governments through mercenaries. You may remember the case of Sir Mark Thatcher, son of former British Prime Minister, Mrs. Margaret Thatcher, who escaped a long jail term in South Africa over a coup plot. As reported in the February 2005 edition of *Africa Today*, Thatcher's arrest by South Africa's elite police unit, the Scorpions, came months after the imprisonment of a group of mercenaries in Zimbabwe led by Simon Mann, and another in Equatorial Guinea, led by Nick du Toit. It later emerged that the two groups were part of a plot, allegedly backed by foreign governments, to topple Teodoro Obiang Nguema Mbasogo, the controversial president of Equatorial Guinea. Reporting on this incident, John Dludlu, writing for *Africa Today*(op cit, 18) stated that Mark Thatcher spoke to the media outside the High Court in Cape Town,"[...]after pleading guilty to charges of bankrolling an alleged coup plot in oil-rich Equatorial Guinea."

In another vein, the recent arrest of nine French nationals in the Republic of Chad charged with child kidnapping is another evidence of the meddling and evil deeds of Westerners and their accessories in Africa. According to *Europe News* (2007:1)

> Six members of Rescue Children and three French journalists were jailed on Thursday on charges of kidnapping and trafficking in children after being taken into custody at the airport of Abeche, in eastern Chad, as they were preparing to leave the country with the children on a Boeing 757 aircraft."

They are suspected of wanting to take the children to France to have them adopted by French families. Chadian President Idriss Deby called the action of the French NGO Rescue Children "inhuman, unacceptable and unthinkable." He said those arrested would be "severely punished", according to *Europe News*. Rescue Children is a French NGO created by the association L'Arche de Zoe, which is run by firefighters in the Paris suburb of Argenteuil. A spokeswoman for the United Nations Children's Fund (UNICEF) Veronique Taveau, speaking in Geneva, said what had happened in Chad and the way it had been carried out was illegal and irresponsible and it had breached all international rules.

The biggest Western myth about Africa is that which regards the continent as one for the taking because of the presumed primitivity and savagery of its people. As Mudimbe (1988:40) has noted, such racist remarks speak neither about Africa nor Africans, but rather justify the process of inventing and conquering a continent and naming its "primitiveness" or "disorder" as well as the subsequent means of its exploitation and methods for its "regeneration." Similarly, Lyons(1975:86-87)notes the consistency with which nineteenth century European commentators regarded Africans as inferior to Whites, quite often comparing the two peoples along the lines of children versus children:

> Though they did agree among themselves about which European "races" were inferior to others, Western racial commentators generally agreed that Blacks were inferior to whites in moral fiber, cultural attainment, and mental ability; the African was, to many eyes, the child in the family of man, modern man in embryo. (Quoted in Booker, 10)

This model of thinking provided a justification for European imperial conquest of Africa. It is interesting to bear in mind that the misrepresentation of Africa constituted a leitmotif in nineteen century European literature. Joseph Conrad's *Heart of Darkness* (1960) is a good example of Western literary texts that paraded racist stereotypes about Africa. Conrad's novel depicts the entire continent as backward and primitive. As Achebe has pointed out:

> *Heart of Darkness* perhaps more than any other work, is informed by a conventional European tendency to set Africa up as a foil to Europe, as a place of negations at once remote and vaguely familiar in comparison with which Europe's own state of spiritual grace will be manifest.(Quoted in Booker, 13)

Like *Heart of Darkness,* many Western literary works about Africa are overtly contemptuous in their racist depictions of Africans. American readers are probably aware of the portrayal of Africans as savage cannibals in Edgar Rice Burroughs's Tarzan novels. But as Booker points out, these writers simply ignored the reality of Africans altogether. The truth of the matter is that the characterization of Africans as cannibals and Africa as an uninhabited wilderness where courageous Europeans could go on exciting adventures, served as justification for the European so-called "civilizing mission" to Africa.

As can be seen, Africa has been victim of Western denigration and tomfoolery for a very long time. Innumerable incidents, including the transportation of millions of Africans across both the Indian and Atlantic Oceans as slaves, the colonial swoop on Africa, and more have produced disastrous effects on the cohesion and productive capacity of African societies. There's an urgent need, I believe, for Africa's historians to assess and write about the horrors suffered by Africans as a result of slavery, racism, colonialism and neo-colonialism. We need these records in order to institute legal proceedings for the payment of reparations to Africa! Memmi (op cit: 91) has pointed out that "the most serious blow suffered by the colonized is being removed from history." This deprivation which produces the stereotypical epithet of Africans as a "people without history," to borrow from Eric Wolf (Quoted in Booker, 25), denies African people access to a usable past from which they can rely in order to construct a viable future. It is critically important for Africans to understand the impact of the continent's past relations with the West in order to empower ourselves to deal effectively with the present. African intellectuals have the duty to educate the people of Africa about the consequences of Western post-colonial meddling in Africa. Europeans and other Western powers continue to mislead and misinform Africans about their own history. Trevor Roper, an eminent English historian at Oxford claims that "prior to European adventure in Africa, there was only darkness, and darkness was not a subject for history."(Quoted in Obiechina, op cit, 9) The onus is on our historians and literati to debunk myths like this one. It is time to call into question the condescending Eurocentric interrogations such as: where would Africa be without Europe? Would African peoples not be half-starving warring tribes eternally at each other's throat fighting for land? We have to desist from feeling permanently injured by a sense of inadequacy about our won achievements. African scholars must be courageous enough to unravel the myth about Africa's collective amnesia. In the words of Ngugi (op cit, 3):

> The classes fighting against imperialism even in its neo-colonial stage and form have to confront this threat with the higher and more creative culture of resolute struggle.

In the wake of the infamous Berlin Conference of 1884, imperialism became a monopolistic parasite, a veritable bugbear of the people of Africa. The Berlin Conference was Africa's undoing in more ways than one. The colonial powers superimposed their hegemony on the African continent. By the time independence returned to Africa the realm had acquired a legacy of political fragmentation that could neither be eliminated nor made to operate satisfactorily.

History has it that on November 15, 1884 at the request of Portugal, German chancellor Otto von Bismarck called together the major Western powers of the world to negotiate the African Question. Bismarck appreciated the opportunity to expand Germany's sphere of influence over Africa and desired to force Germany's rivals to struggle with one another for territory. What ultimately resulted was a hodgepodge of geometric boundaries that divided Africa into fifty irregular countries. This new map of the continent was superimposed over the one thousand indigenous cultures and regions of Africa. The new countries lacked rhyme or reason because European powers had divided coherent groups of people and merged together disparate groups who really did not get along. Little wonder that post-Berlin Africa has remained a battlefield to date. The debilitating effects of imperialism on the lives of Africans are real. In the words of Ngugi (op cit, 2):

> Imperialism is total: it has economic, political, military, cultural and psychological consequences for the people of the world today. It could even lead to a holocaust.

In this essay, I have attempted to trace the genesis of Africa's collective woes to the 1884 Berlin Conference where nascent imperialism occasioned the partition of Africa. I have further imputed the present state of underdevelopment and instability in Africa not to Africa's collective amnesia of the horrors of the past but to the overt and covert machinations of Western powers on the African continent.

Chapter Ten
A CONTINENT'S DIRTY LINEN

The geographical expression called Niger Republic is the shame of the African continent. After outlawing slavery a couple of years ago and making this shameful practice a crime punishable with up to 30 years in prison, the government of this tiny desert country lacks the courage to implement its own laws. What appears to have happened in Niger is that the government, despite passing a law against slave-ownership, has been embarrassed by revelations by international human rights groups such as Anti-Slavery International who have reported that at least 43,000 people are thought to be enslaved in the Republic of Niger at present. The anti-slavery law has made little difference in remote parts of the country where callous individuals, notably chieftains continue to trade in human "cargo".

The irksome thing about what is going on in Niger is the fact that the country's leadership seems to be unperturbed. The head of state and his henchmen have been trying to shy away from the responsibility of cracking down on slave-owners. Sadly enough, this is happening at a time when Niger is the focus of heightened international attention. The country has just taken over the presidency of the Economic Community of West African States (ECOWAS). It is also playing host to the fifth *Francophonie* Games. One would like to know what the international community is doing in order to effectively put an end to the rape of humanity that is going on in Niger. One wonders why the head of State cannot respect the oath he took upon coming to office to protect the supreme law of the land. Every president, I presume, has the duty to protect the national constitution. Why is this not happening in Niger? These are burning questions that citizens of this impoverished nation should be posing. How long shall Africa and the rest of the world stand idly and watch callous individuals perpetrate diabolical acts on the continent with impunity? What does it take to galvanize the people of Niger out of their slumber into open rebellion against a culture that has brought so much opprobrium upon their country and the African continent as a whole? The African Union, ECOWAS and Western donors should be putting pressure on the government of Niger to right the wrongs of the past or be subjected to financial asphyxiation? Sadly enough, there is no crude oil in this country to attract global attention.

Another country that poses a similar threat to the stability of Africa is the tiny Republic of Togo. This country is notorious for its child trafficking practices. Writing in the August 2005 edition of *Africa Today*, the editor (2005:21) pointed out that Human Rights Watch (HRW) defines child trafficking as: "the recruitment, transportation and harboring of children for purposes of sexual or labor exploitation. Child exploitation is a growing concern not just in Togo but on the entire African continent. Abject poverty has driven some families to sell their own children into slavery. Statistics from the Togolese Social Affairs Ministry indicate that about 3000 children have been transported across the Togolese border with neighboring countries. The question that begs asking is what has been done by the Togolese law enforcement officials to punish perpetrators of this heinous crime.

The United States of America has warned Togo and other countries involved in this odious trade to end it or face severe consequences. One only hopes that the US will follow through with this threat. Apparently, the menace from Americans has galvanized the paranoic Togolese government into action. Recently, the parliament passed a law that spells out sanctions relating to child-trafficking. Children's rights groups believe that the recent legislation in Togo constitutes a significant step toward eradicating a practice that has brought much disgrace on the African continent. Other countries should take their cue from Togo.

Chapter Eleven
PHANTOMS OF THE PAST

One of the contraptions conceived by the West to subjugate Africans was the myth about Africa's barbarity. The white man arrogated upon himself the task of bringing light to the so-called "dark" continent. Africans were perceived as a benighted savage cannibalistic bunch of people devoid of civilization. However, underlying this seeming benevolence was the belief that the African continent would become a source of raw materials to feed Western industries. The lust for wealth engulfed even some European priests, who abandoned their evangelizing mission, took black women as concubines, kept slaves themselves, and sold their "converts" into slavery. Unaware of the evil deeds of these self-styled missionaries, Africans continued to revere them; oblivious of the fact that these priests were actually ancillaries of the colonial administration.

Mongo Beti has described the "civilizing mission" as a gigantic western scheme used as a ploy to dispossess Africans not only of their wealth but also of their cultural identity. As Bjornson (1991:328) has pointed out:

> By unmasking the self-serving rhetoric that obscures the nature of neo-colonialist exploitation, Beti proposed to destroy the credibility of this false image.

Beti argues that every African intellectual has an obligation to foster the culture of his people and to control its image because those who fail to do so will fall prey to the bluff about the superiority of the white man's culture. What he means by "culture" is not an outmoded set of superstitions but rather the actual life and aspirations of the people.

Hoodwinked by the white man's self-proclaimed superiority over the dark race, Africans and people of African descent have failed to realize that the West harbors its own savages and cannibals? In other words, what has been brandished as modernism in the West is only a façade calculated to shroud the barbaric nature of Westerners. If you take a walk down memory lane and recall the genocide of the American Indians, you would agree with the point I am trying to make. The story of the encounter between European settlers and America's native population does not make for pleasant reading. Among early accounts, perhaps the most famous is Helen Hunt Jackson's *A Century of Dishonor* (1888), a doleful recitation of forced removals, killings, and callous disregard. Jackson's book clearly captures some essential elements of what happened.

Another scholar that has written about the genocide of native Americans is Ward Churchill, a professor of ethnic studies at the University of Colorado. He contends that the reduction of the North American Indian population from an estimated 12 million in 1500 to barely 237,000 in 1900 represents a "vast genocide [...] the most sustained on record."(Quoted in Lewy,1) By the end of the 19th century, writes David E. Stannard, a historian at the University of Hawaii, native Americans had undergone the "worst human holocaust the world had ever witnessed, roaring across two continents non-stop for four centuries and consuming the lives of countless tens of millions of people."(Quoted in Lewy,1) In the judgment of Lenore A. Stiffarm and Phil Lane, Jr., "there can be no more monumental example of sustained genocide—certainly none involving a "race" of people as broad and complex as this—anywhere in the annals of human history."(Quoted in Lewy,1) I have singled out the American Indian Holocaust for discussion because of the importance of America in the game of pace-setting on the globe. The West is replete with similar histories.

More recently, in July 20, 2004, the 'Associated Press' carried a headline story of a cannibal resident in Kansas city in the United States of America. The paper reported that on July 23, 2004, twenty-five year-old Marc Sappington was convicted of murdering three acquaintances, including a teenager whose body was dismembered and partially eaten. The cannibal pleaded guilty on murder charges as well as one count each of kidnapping and aggravated burglary stemming from a separate carjacking.

Sappington told the court that voices ordered him to kill and eat Terry Green, 25, Michael Weaver Jr., 22 and Alton Fred Brown 16, over a four-day span in April 2001. He further asserted that the voices he heard told him he had to eat human flesh and drink human blood or he would die—voices he said he only heard when he was high on the hallucinogenic drug called PCP. Your take on this issue is as good as mine. Needless to say that it is high time Africans embarked on a philanthropic "civilizing mission" to the West.

Chapter Twelve
PATH TO REBIRTH

The term "renaissance'" has come to mean different things to different people. In this light, it is necessary to put the expression into perspective. *The New Encyclopedia Britannica* defines "renaissance" as: "rebirth, the period in European civilization immediately following the Middle ages, conventionally held to have been characterized by a surge of interest in classical learning and values." (1019) It was in arts that the spirit of renaissance achieved its sharpest formulation. Art came to be seen as a branch of knowledge, valuable in its own right. If something experiences a renaissance, it becomes popular again after a time when people had lost interest in it.

As products of Western educational systems, most educated Africans straddle Europe and Africa; indigenous and Western traditions. For the sake of survival in a globalizing economy, Africans have no choice but to embrace Western civilization. This must be done, I believe, within the context of African indigenous cultures. Echoing Mongo Beti's stance on this issue, Bjornson (op cit, 105) observes:

> Beti's point is that Africans will never enjoy true
> freedom until they learn how to interpret the
> modern world and take the initiative for making
> it their own. (105)

Africans have a rich culture of care, mutual respect, self-esteem, love and protection. Childcare for instance, is not perceived by Africans as the duty of the child's biological parents alone. It is seen as a communal responsibility involving members of the nuclear and extended families. That explains why in Africa the young address the elderly as "Pa" or "Ma" regardless of blood relationship. By the same token, the elderly address the young as "son" or "daughter" whether they are biologically related or not.

Africans possess time-honored methods of inculcating moral values and life skills into their offspring. This is a task that begins at birth and continues into adulthood. This preservation of cultural heritage is, to my mind, a manifestation of African renaissance which makes African cultures distinct from other world cultures. Espousing the concept of African renaissance is tantamount to embracing those elements of African cultures that would identify us as a people with a common heritage. African renaissance, I think, is the quest for a modus operandi that would enable African parents, community leaders, teachers and social workers to instill into children respect for cultural values. Renaissance amounts to a revalorization of our customs and traditions. It needs to be pointed out that this does not presuppose the rejection of the cultures of others because Africans do not believe in exclusion. Accepting the ideals of African renaissance will equip us with the tools necessary to take our destiny into our own hands. At the same time, African renaissance should not be construed as a negation of our Western educational baggage. Certainly, Africans can enjoy the best of both worlds, for the simple reason that most of us are products of both Western and African educational systems. The onus is on us, I think, to preserve our African cultural values and pass them down to the younger generation. We must teach our children to be to proud of their African identity: languages, styles of dress, cuisine, ceremonies, etc. We must teach them to be respectful of others. We must teach them to steer clear of hate speech and violence.

In the past, cultural education was seen as the preserve of parents. Not any more. It is high time Africans started to think about transposing cultural education into the school arena. We could get started by Africanizing school curricula. This may sound like a pipe-dream but you know what, if Dr Martin Luther King did not dream, African Americans would still be riding in the back of buses in the land of their birth today! If Nelson Mandela did not dream, black South Africans would still be confined to Bantu education today! So let's not be afraid of our own dreams. We must not lose sight of the fact that necessity is the mother of invention. In brief, as we continue to celebrate our dual heritage we should not forget the daunting task that lies ahead of us. It is not a task for outsiders. It is ours!

Chapter Thirteen
HITLER IN AFRICA

Led by Adolf Hitler, the Nazis committed unpardonable crimes against humanity many years ago. The tragic event has been described by historians as the Holocaust—the systematic, bureaucratic, state-sponsored persecution and murder of millions of Jews by the Nazi regime and its collaborators. "Holocaust" is a word of Greek origin meaning "sacrifice by fire." The Nazis, who came to power in Germany in January 1933, believed that Germans were racially superior and that the Jews, deemed inferior, were an alien threat to the so-called German racial community.

During the era of the Holocaust, German authorities also targeted other groups because of their perceived racial inferiority, namely Roma (Gypsies), the disabled, and some of the Slavic peoples (Poles, Russians, and others). Other groups were persecuted on political, ideological, and behavioral grounds, among them Communists, Socialists, Jehovah's Witnesses, and homosexuals. Fuelled by hatred for the Jews, the Nazis exterminated approximately six million Jews in gas chambers.

More than half a century after this gruesome tragedy, a calamity of almost similar magnitude has transpired, this time on the African continent. Not long ago, the Hutu of Rwanda agreed that the Tutsi, ethnically related to the Banyamulenge of Zaire, now called the Democratic Republic of Congo (DRC), were 'cockroaches'. This meant that the Tutsi were an inferior ethnic group and had to be eliminated. They did not deserve to live! Strong in their conviction, the Hutu carried out a genocide that left the entire world astounded. The Rwandan genocide remains an indelible dark spot on the image of Africa. The bloodbath that lasted 100 days took away the lives of a million people!

On Friday August 13, 2004 a similar incident occurred in a refugee camp in Gatumba in Burundi, where ethnic cleansers headed by a self-proclaimed born-again Christian and leader of the Palipehutu-FNL party, murdered in cold blood well over 150 children, women and men in their sleep. The Palipehutu-FNL leader was elected president of Burundi in a poll organized in 2005! Needless to say history holds a lot in store for us.

The genocide in Darfur, Sudan is blood curdling. The whole world was shocked by the bloodbath orchestrated by a bunch of demented militias calling themselves the *Jajaweed*. The Darfur genocide has resulted in the death of more than 400,000 civilians and the displacement of 2.5 million people from their homes. The ongoing Darfur Genocide is no accident. It is the brutal plan of three men in the Sudanese national government. Yet Western governments continue to cut deals with them. In February 2003, frustrated by poverty and neglect, two Darfurian rebel groups launched an uprising against the Khartoum government. The government responded with a scorched-earth campaign, arming and bankrolling militias against the innocent civilians of Darfur. It is time the US and European governments stopped appeasing genocide and fully support the International Criminal Court to indict the perpetrators of genocide on the African continent. It is time for justice, because only justice can bring peace. A small peacekeeping force run by the African Union is in place, but it is largely unsupported by the rest of the world. Civilian protection is desperately needed to stop the violence and end the genocide.

This writer wonders why the African Union and the United Nations have not taken bold action to halt the carnage on the African continent. Most importantly, one would like to know when Africans would learn to love one another and stop portraying ourselves to the global community as a bunch of demented blood-thirsty barbarians.

Chapter Fourteen
APORIA: AFRICA'S DEMO-DICTATORS

It is tempting to dismiss numerous complaints about abuse of power in Africa as the ranting of Afro-pessimists. But come to think of it, the continent is replete with demo-dictators, compulsive megalomaniacs who are simply obsessed with power. Africa's so-called political leaders have made it clear, in word and deed, that they would stop at nothing in their attempt to monopolize political power in perpetuity. Sometimes it feels like these leaders are addicted to power. In a bid to stay in power until death do them part, it has now become common practice for African heads of state to tinker with national constitutions.

Former President Sam Nujoma of Namibia is a case in point. This man toyed with the supreme law of the land as if he were a child playing around with toys. Each time his term of office came close to expiration, Nujoma simply tweaked the constitution in order to give himself another term of office. According to Amupadhi (2004:1), the situation was so bad in the days of Nujoma that the Congress of Democrats (CoD) called the President a "political trickster" and Swapo a "circus of magicians". Ben Ulenga, president of the CoD observes that "... Namibians had for the past 14 years been tricked and bamboozled into electing false leaders who had failed to deliver on visions of the [...] Biblical Promised Land." He further notes that Swapo had destroyed the educational system and was taking Namibia backward into something worse than a banana republic. It is the hope of this writer that incumbent president Hifikepunye Pohamba has not learned Nujoma's dirty tricks.

President Paul Biya of Cameroon is ruling another puppet republic. He is notorious for his political tricksterism. This man with a squeaky voice came to power in 1982, from the position of Prime minister, after purportedly colluding with the French to oust President Ahmadou Ahidjo. Twenty-six years after this political watershed, Mr. Biya is still hanging onto executive power in Cameroon! He resorts to heavy-handed repression and torture in order to silence dissenting voices in the country. Cameroonians of some thinking capacity have identified corruption as the scourge of the nation thanks to Biya's wheeling and dealing with his "Ali Baba gang" of thieving ministers. The president simply turns a blind eye to the heinous crimes committed by his ministers on a daily basis. Rather than confront corruption head on, he continues to chase shadows. Biya seems to be a firm believer in the *Francophonie* dictum which says that "La chèvre broute là où elle est attachée" [The goat eats where it is tethered.] He honestly believes that he can fool Cameroonians and the international community with his simulations, half-truths, and cosmetic solutions to the nation's myriad problems. This is a leader that is so loathed by the populace that his death would be welcome news nationwide.

In 2005, news about his untimely demise flashed through the front pages of local newspapers in Cameroon. The nation went berserk in jubilation thinking that God had finally provided the long-awaited biological solution to their insurmountable problems, only to find out that it was a yarn spun by an opponent of the President resident in the United States of America (strangely enough, a native of Mr. president's own Beti tribe). If the unpopularity of a political leader is anything to go by, you have got it! Mismanagement, lack of accountability, loss of confidence in state political and economic institutions, seclusion and manipulation of the people based on political affiliations, and a repressive law enforcement machinery are the collection of factors that account for the hatred that Cameroonians nurse against their president.

There have been allegations in the past of his plotting to have his snipers assassinate Christian Cardinal Tumi (the representative of the Vatican in Cameroon). Cardinal Tumi is reputed for his acerbic diatribes against President Biya's inanity and bad governance. The situation is so bad in Cameroon that the Belgium-based branch of the Southern Cameroons National Conference (SCNC) has dispatched a petition containing an extensive list of human rights abuses committed by Biya and his lieutenants to the UN Secretary-General. The petitioners are calling upon the UN boss to set up a tribunal for the trial of Paul Biya for crimes against humanity. The petitioners also request the assistance of the UN in the peaceful restoration of the Statehood of the Southern Cameroons.

Biya is notorious for rigging elections at the expense of opposition parties in the country. As Ngwane (2008:6) has pointed out:

> In effect there are a lot of exogenous factors that deprive the Opposition from starting the election race on the same block as the ruling party—disenfranchisement, nonchalant international community, low civic participation, mass rigging…

The recent unrest that has led to several casualties in Cameroon stems from the fact that Mr. Biya is open to the idea of a Constitutional amendment that would allow him to run for re-election in 2011. He basically sees no end to his stay in power, despite the fact that his regime has been responsible for dilapidating the nation's wealth and viability, while remaining a constant source of terror and human rights violations. Even though the idea of a constitutional amendment is very unpopular from every indication throughout the national territory, Paul Biya seems to be counting on the support of the CPDM-dominated National Assembly to review the constitution and effect the necessary amendments necessary to enable him to remain in power for live!

Next door to Cameroon, another demo-dictator El Hadj Omar Bongo Ondimba, born Albert-Bernard Bongo, is hanging onto power in Gabon. Bongo, Africa's longest serving president came to power in November 1967, and has remained president of this country to date! Under the 1961 constitution (revised in 1975, rewritten in 1991, and revised in 2003), the president can appoint and dismiss the prime minister, the cabinet, and judges of the "independent" Supreme Court. The president also has other strong powers, such as authority to dissolve the National Assembly, declare a state of siege, delay legislation, and conduct referenda. A 2003 constitutional amendment removed presidential term limits and facilitated a presidency for life. As Celestin Monga (1997:1) has pointed out, "...it is hard, if not impossible, to persuade Africa's authoritarian leaders to accept democratic rules." Attempts to cover up administrative incompetence have become the hallmark of Bongo who does not hesitate to menace political opponents. His government is riddled with corruption.

Kenyan President Mwai Kibaki is another budding dictator on the African continent. He is not faring well during his tenure given that he is not comfortable with democratic tenets. The recent election violence that came in the wake of the rigged presidential election in the county not long ago where over 800 people have been killed lends ample credence to this fact. The violence continues to date. Large numbers of ethnic hackings, rapes, and murders have followed. The question that begs to be asked is what set off this madness? Kibaki probably lost the vote to opposition leader Raila Odinga by about 8%, according to exit polls conducted by Washington-based International Republican Institute, but Kibaki claimed a 3% victory over Odinga. According to Travis Kavulla, (2008:2)"... a terrible blow has been dealt to what seemed to be one of Africa's most sophisticated democracies." The protests of American, European, and South African election monitors against the election result have gone unheeded. Kibaki simply had a good laugh from being accused by Americans of rigging elections.

The situation in Zimbabwe is pathetic. Robert Mugabe continues to behave like a demented person. He became Zimbabwe's political leader in 1980 after independence elections, and was hailed as a model African democrat. The former Marxist guerrilla has held fast to power despite deep political and economic crises that threaten to ruin the country he fought so hard to set free from Western imperialism. His tyrannical buffoonery is affecting not only the economy of Zimbabwe but also that of the entire Southern African Development Community (SADC) sub-region. After making a fool of himself during the civil war in the Democratic Republic of Congo (DRC), Mugabe has now turned to his own compatriots to vent his ire. His land redistribution program has proven to be a complete fiasco! The land he grabs from detested white farmers is not given to Zimbabweans in dire need of farmland; rather it is given to the president's cronies and sweethearts! Disinherited Zimbabweans who really need farm-land remain landless. It would appear that Mugabe has outlived his usefulness as a political leader. Common sense dictates that we make way for others when we are a spent force. I believe that Mugabe is at the helm of a political system that has fallen out of touch with the needs of the masses. The lack of vision exhibited by this African leader adds to the misery of Zimbabweans. Mugabe lacks foresight as far as the future of his country is concerned. He should be wise enough, I argue, to relinquish power before it is wrested from his hands. The list of Africa's demo-dictators is interminable. Here and there one runs into a fawning political "acrobat" who says one thing and does the exact opposite.

Yoweri Museveni of Uganda, once revered as Africa's visionary, has joined the gang of political jugglers. Museveni became president in January 1986 after seizing Kampala following a five-year guerrilla struggle. He banned multi-party politics shortly afterwards. In July 2005, sensing that his second and last term was coming to an end, he quickly persuaded the parliament dominated by his henchmen to lift the presidential term limits from the constitution in order to give him the chance to run for the presidency for the third time! It should be remembered that when Museveni came to power in 1986; he promptly outlawed multiparty politics, saying it was divisive. Not long after the pronouncement the same man was out in the streets of Kampala calling upon Ugandans to vote for multiparty politics in a referendum. Ugandans must be very confused!

The question of misgovernment in Africa has reached such crisis proportions that African literati have taken it upon themselves to fictionalize it. Ghanaian novelist and poet Kofi Awoonor has fictionalized the Question of Power in Africa in his novel titled *This Earth, My Brother* (1972). Awoonor's novel depicts the disintegration of post-independence Africa under demo-dictators in the form of a kaleidoscopic view of African society as it passes from colonial bondage to freedom and self-determination, and finally to a new form of bondage in the hands of its new African leaders. The novelist's deepest emotions are disgust, anger and despair at the betrayal of the ideals of democracy and the aspirations of the newly independent African states. The reader is made to feel that change in Africa is cosmetic; only an illusion. The history of African societies, Awoonor seems to say, is a vicious circle of exploitation of the ordinary people, first by white masters and then by the black surrogates. He is certainly a vigorous critic of the inept political leadership in contemporary Africa, of the shallow philistinism of the new ruling class.

In a similar vein, Kenyan novelist and dramatist Ngugi wa Thiong'o has lambasted Kenyan petit bourgeoisie in his novel *Petals of Blood*(1977).In this novel, Ngugi wonders aloud about the problems of modern Africa: the sharp divide between the ill-gotten wealth of the new African middle-class and the worsening plight of the unemployed and peasants. He expresses his disenchantment with post-independence Kenya and the betrayal of the people by the ruling elite.

Disillusionment with post-independence Nigeria forms the subject of Chinua Achebe's novel *A man of the People(1966)*. Achebe debunks the myth of independence in Africa by telling the story of Chief Nanga, one-time school teacher who becomes the Honorable Minister of Culture. Nanga is corrupt to the core as are most of our leaders in Africa. He is portrayed as a prototype of the African politician who takes the people for a ride.

In a similar vein, Ayi Kwei Armah's *The Beautyful Ones Are Not Yet Born* (1968) is a scathing satire of corruption, moral decadence and abuse of power in Ghana of the 1960s. The novel portrays what Booker (1998: x) sees as "an entire society overwhelmed by corruption brought about primarily with fascination with the 'gleam' of Western commodity culture."

This notwithstanding, it is heartening to know that there are a few good leaders in Africa. Festus Gontebanye Mogae of Botswana, educated at oxford, majoring in economics, is a role model. His country is a success story in Africa, economically speaking. He has achieved the best economic growth rate in the past couple of years. One wonders what magic potion he employs to achieve such sterling results. His peers would do well to learn from him.

President Thabo Mbeki of South Africa, I believe, is another success story. He confronts corruption head on! His recent firing of his own corrupt deputy, Jacob Zuma, bears testimony to his zero tolerance commitment to tackling corruption in the country. After Nelson Mandela's exit from the presidency in 1998, the world held its breath in anticipation of what South Africa would become. President Mbeki has proven skeptics wrong. Suffice it to say that all is not lost on the African continent. Africa may be saddled with corrupt politicians, yet there is light at the end of the tunnel.

All in all, in this paper, I have argued that our political leaders are our arch-enemies. They double-speak, cheat, lie and play games. Kowtowing to their self-serving dictates would spell doom for Africa. As Ngugi wa Thiong'o has pointed out in his novel *Matigari* (1989) subservience to demo-dictators is tantamount to robotic sycophancy which he refers to as "parrotology". At its most obnoxious level, "parrotology" is associated with the intellectuals and the news media personnel, all of whom make the reign of dictatorship possible.

Chapter Fifteen
AFRICA'S TSUNAMI

When cataclysmic incidents like tsunami (the undersea earthquake that hit the peoples of Asia very hard) happen, one is bound to take a second look at the situation back in Africa where many countries have been hit as well by natural disasters. Countries like Gabon, Cameroon, Niger and Ivory Coast among others have been affected by natural disasters yet very little action has been taken to prevent future occurrences. Ethiopia, which is on the verge of famine, has accused the world of waiting until skeletons appear on its television screens before taking action. While Ethiopia was grappling unnoticed with its drought vast areas of Mozambique disappeared under floodwaters. A woman gave birth to a child in a tree during one of those floods! According to a report by UNICEF Mozambique (2008:1) "Rosita Pedro became a baby celebrity when she was born up a tree as her mother sought refuge from the rising waters. Rosita and her mother, 26-year-old Sofia Pedro were winched by a helicopter rescue team to safety, and to some stardom." God really has uncanny ways of doing things.

Even if drought and floods are unpredictable in themselves, they happen with a predictable regularity. So why is the response to such natural disasters frequently so slow in Africa? Africa's political leadership continues to pay scant attention to the impact of environmental degradation on local economies. Poor people all over Africa are vulnerable to droughts and floods since they depend on rainfed agriculture as their main means of subsistence and often live in degraded areas susceptible to rainfall variation. As I see it, there appear to be two main problems related to disaster management in Africa: the piecemeal approach to funding and a lack of co-ordination between governments and aid agencies. Inattention to environmental degradation in Africa has been attributed to environmental illiteracy which has resulted in the indiscriminate exploitation of meager natural resources by impoverished communities. Most Africans abuse the natural environment in the struggle to eke out a subsistence living through agricultural activities, many of which are detrimental to the health of the ecosystem. Human beings and the natural environment, I believe, are on a collision course. Human activities inflict harsh and often irreparable damage on the physical environment and natural resources. It should be noted that if this lackluster attitude toward environmental protection goes on unchecked many of our current practices will put the future generations of Africans at risk for many years to come.

Sadly enough, when environmental and energy interests clash in the West, Africa goes up in flames, the same flames that dot the landscape of our oil-wells. The vendetta between MOSOP (Movement for the Survival of Ogoni People), the organization led by late Ken Saro Wiwa, is a case in point. I was in Nigeria on November 10, 1995 when the military dictatorship of General Sani Abacha, at the peak of international criticism of Nigeria's despotic regime ordered that Saro Wiwa and eight others (the "Ogoni Nine" be executed by hanging. This was done by military personnel after a sham trial condemned as "judicial murder" by Britain's Prime Minister at the time, John Major. Saro Wiwa's real crime had been his defiance of the British oil giant, Shell BP, and one of Africa's most brutal military dictators, Sani Abacha. According to most accounts, Ken's death provoked international outrage and the immediate suspension of Nigeria from the Commonwealth of Nations, which was meeting in New Zealand at the time.

Saro Wiwa and his followers were from Ogoniland, a small densely populated region of the Niger Delta, where Shell had found oil in the 1950's. While the company had grown rich from the profits extracted from the Delta, the local communities continued to live in abject poverty, lacking basic facilities such as good roads, schools, healthcare and clean water. *Africa Today* (2005:1) points out that during a mass protest against the spoliation of their land by Shell BP, Saro Wiwa was noted to have said:

> The march is against the devastation of the environment. It is against the non-payment of royalties. It is anti-Shell. It is anti-federal government, because as far as we are concerned the two are in league to destroy the Ogoni people.

Views like these placed Saro Wiwa and his Ogoni followers at loggerheads with the military junta headed by Abacha. The animosity resulted in repeated detention, torture and murder. Rowell (2005:2) of *Africa Today* notes:

> In the ten years since their deaths, little has changed in the Niger Delta. Oil remains a curse. The communities are still locked into a cycle of extreme poverty, widespread unemployment, environmental pollution and social injustice that has increasingly manifested itself in violent conflict.

The need for sustainable exploitation of Africa's natural resources has been articulated in quite a few policy documents in Africa. In these documents there's been a persistent call for educating people on environmental sustainability and sustainable development. Education for sustainable development would equip Africans with the knowledge, skills, values and attitudes necessary to cater for their present needs while leaving a healthy environment behind for future generations. This is what has been described by UNESCO (2004:72) as "education for sustainable living." The organization points out that sustainable development "meets the needs of present generations without compromising the ability of future generations to meet their own needs." There is a dire need for sustainability education in Africa as we struggle to take up the challenge posed by natural disasters and also to provide a viable environment for the generations that will come after us. What we need to do at this juncture is educate our people on the need for environmental protection. To achieve this objective, we need to give priority to environmental education for sustainability.

I have the conviction that it would be rewarding for education policy-makers on the continent to consider including environmental education in school curricula. The government of South Africa, I believe, is right on track in this respect. The constitution of this country has a clause on environmental protection. Furthermore, secondary and post-secondary education policy-makers place a high priority on environmental preservation. South Africa has signed at least twenty-four major international agreements concerning environmental preservation, including the 1973 Convention on International Trade in Endangered Species of Wild Fauna and Flora (CITES) and the 1987 Protocol on Substances that Deplete the Ozone Layer, or Montreal Protocol. The government's Council on the Environment has proposed a new approach to environmental preservation called Integrated Environmental Management, aimed at accommodating development concerns. The 1989 legislation and subsequent amendments set out the official objectives in environmental conservation--to preserve species and ecosystems, to maintain ecological processes, and to fight against land degradation and environmental deterioration resulting from human activities. The government of South Africa requires environmental impact assessments (EIAs) for major development and construction projects, and it imposes fines on industrial polluters. I believe that the example of South Africa should be emulated by all African countries.

In this essay, I have attempted to shed light on the impact of natural disasters on Africa's physical and built environments. I have also endeavored to speculate on the wide-ranging implications of inadequate disaster management on the economies and politics of nation-states. I argue that environmental disasters constitute the "tragedy of the commons," using the word "tragedy" as the philosopher Whitehead used it to refer to the fact that the essence of dramatic tragedy is not unhappiness. It resides in the solemnity of the remorseless working of things. In other words, there is a subset of problems, such as population, atomic war, environmental corruption, and the recovery of a livable urban environment that threaten the very existence of contemporary man.

Chapter Sixteen
RITE OF PASSAGE OR UNSAFE ORDEAL

Africa is replete with customs and traditions that need to be revisited and challenged. Such is the case with the rite of passage, or what many Africans call the "circumcision school".

Circumcision is a practice whereby the loose foreskin at the end of a boy's penis is cut off. The Akamba and the Massai, in East Africa, are just two groups where circumcision of boys is the central rite of passage. In South Africa and Bukusuland, which covers mainly the western Kenyan districts of Bungoma and Tran-Nzoia, circumcision is a huge event which as Eric Maino (2002:2) puts it, is characterized by "excessive consumption of traditional liquor and hard drugs such as marijuana, as people sing and dance." In some cultures, girls are circumcised too. The Nandi in Kenya, for example, have their girls circumcised in a long drawn out ceremony. There is much emphasis on bravery and enduring pain without complaint. The rationale behind this age-old custom remains unclear to many outsiders. Nonetheless, Africans who cling tenaciously onto the practice claim that circumcision is a sacred rite of passage. It is of interest to note that the human cycle of birth, growing up, marriage and death is marked all the way with religious observances in Africa. The transition from childhood to adulthood in traditional African societies is carefully marked and charted.

Pro-circumcision activists contend that the practice is an inevitable passage from childhood to adulthood. In other words, it is the bridge between the child and the man. It is thus a test of endurance. As Maino points out(op cit, 2), "The young boy, who stays in the deep night's cold without wearing a shirt, blows a whistle, and knocks two metal pieces with sisal whiskers at the end(*chinyimba*) to rhythmically hit iron bangles worn on the hand. As a test of him withstanding the blade the following morning, he is abused and wiped (sic), while others go an extra mile to place hot iron metal on his toe nails [...] Very early in the morning the initiate is circumcised naked in the presence of the entire society..." Despite the brutality associated with the rite of circumcision, many Africans still uphold the practice. Mpho Mphahlele, a senior at Meridian High School-Pietersburg in South Africa, feels very strongly about the practice of circumcision. He is heir to the throne of Ga-Mphahlele village. He maintains:

> I don't see why we should abolish the rite of circumcision. It is a custom that was passed

> down to us by our fore-fathers. It is our duty to
> also hand it down to our own children
> (Interview by author, April 2, 2002).

The initiation school is viewed by others as a nursery where moral rectitude is inculcated into youths. During their sojourn in the bushes, elders teach the initiates courage, patience, resilience and endurance. Another life skill that is instilled in them during the initiation ritual is creative thinking. They are taught to think on their feet. As a result of the various ordeals to which they are subjected at the initiation school: poor feeding, lack of water, occasional corporal punishment, loss of blood, mosquito bite and chilly nights, the children develop quick-witted problem-solving skills. Most importantly, the initiation school is seen as a test of manhood. Speaking during an interview, Michael Ngoetjana admits:

> In the village of Ga-Mashashane it is absolutely
> impossible to find a girl to marry if you didn't
> graduate from the circumcision school
> (Interview by author, August 15, 2003).

From the foregoing, it is clear that the rite of initiation is one of the most controversial traditions in Africa. There is a sizeable number of dissenting voices. These include people who believe that the initiation school is an evil. Wilson Sekepe, a teacher at Capricorn High School in Pietersburg, feels strongly about the harm done to children by the initiation school:

> Circumcision is a barbaric act that harms young
> children physically and mentally. Some children
> lose their penises in the process on account of
> the unhealthy habits that prevail at the initiation
> school (Interview by author, November 30, 2002).

Sekepe adds that circumcision sometimes interferes with the reproductive system of children who go through the school. Besides, some of them feel raped after circumcision. This feeling remains with them for life. Other teachers complain that the initiation school disrupts the formal schooling of children and contributes to the high dropout rates in South African schools. Mohamadou Koné, biology teacher at Taxila High School in Pietersburg, expressed his reservations as follows:

> Kids undergoing initiation stay away from
> school for a period of three months! How on
> earth are they expected to catch up with their
> studies after spending so much time out of
> school? (Interview by author, June 22, 2002).

Environmental activists have their own list of grievances against the initiation school. They believe that some activities associated with initiation are harmful to the environment. For example, trees are cut down for firewood during the initiation season. Soil erosion is aggravated by the uprooting of trees and birds are deprived of their natural habitat. Worse still, accidental bushfires destroy topsoil and plant nutrients. Biodiversity is threatened by occasional soil pollution. There is also noise pollution produced by the screaming boys.

In a nutshell, the initiation school is perceived as unfriendly to the environment. Initiation does not only harm the health of the environment. It harms the health of the children as well. As Maino (op cit, 2) has pointed out: the widely practiced tradition of circumcising boys is now seen as a threat to life. The use of the same circumcision knife to operate on several initiates has increased the chances of transmitting viruses, including HIV [...] During the process; the same knife is stained with blood. When used on another boy, chances are high that some viruses including HIV could be easily transmitted." Grace Sedibana, a social worker in Hammanskraal, has similar concerns:

> In the village of Hammanskraal, we are saddened by the prevalence of HIV-AIDS transmitted from child to child at the initiation school (Interview by author, March 9, 2003)

Grace is horrified that witchdoctors use the same knife to circumcise scores of children.

All in all, the debate on the rite of initiation is ongoing in Africa, the more so because this custom has its merits and demerits. Whether it should be proscribed or not remains a bone of contention.

NOTES

[1] Police officer noted for extorting money from taxi drivers.
[2] Police force in the French-speaking region of Cameroon and other francophone countries.
[3] Anglophones are clumsy
[4] They are enemies in the house.
[5] They are Biafrans
[6] Native name of Cameroon.
[7] Though francophone, the Bamileke have more in common, culturally-speaking, with English-speaking compatriots than they do with French-speaking Cameroonians.
[8] Tailored to meet the needs of French-speaking Cameroonians.
[9] Poem published in the author's poetry anthology, *African Time and Pidgin Verses,* Duplico, 2001.
[10] This man is uncivilized; he can't speak English.
[11] *La Francophonie* is an international organization of French-speaking countries and governments. Formally known as the *Organisation internationale de la Francophonie* (OIF) or the International Organization of La Francophonie, the organisation comprises fifty-five member states and governments and thirteen observers. The prerequisite for admission is not the degree of French usage in the member countries, but a prevalent presence of French culture and French language in the member country's identity, usually stemming from France's interaction with other nations in its history.
[12] Annual reed dance
[13] Bride price
[14] *The Suns of Independence,* p.20.
[15] Mistresses
[16] *The Second Sex* , p.267
[17] Op cit., p.427
[18] Retrogressive attitude
[19] No time to rest; our days are numbered.
[20] Shortened form of the word "*mbutuku*", that refers to "a good-for-nothing person, "a weakling" or "an idiot". Mainly used by young people, this loanword exists in Cameroon Pidgin English since the 1970s.
[21] Published in the author's anthology of poems titled *African Time and Other verses,* Duplico, 2001.
[22] The term is sometimes used to refer to lower classes of the bourgeoisie.

[23] The Lilliputians symbolize humankind's wildly excessive pride in its own puny existence. Swift fully intends the irony of representing the tiniest race.
[24] The best pupil of President François Mitterrand
[25] Any person of mixed ancestry
[26] Presidential palace
[27] The worst has come to the worst!

Works cited

Abusharaf, Mustapha, R. (2006). *Female Circumcision: Multiple Perspectives*. Philadelphia: University of Pennsylvania Press.

Achebe, Chinua. (1966). *A Man of the People*. London: Heinemann.

Akpata-Ohohe, Bunmi (2005). 'The magnificent Baaba Maal.' *Africa Today*, 11, 35-38.

Amupadhi, Tangeni. (2004). 'Swapo has led Country to Economic and Social Destruction.' June 14, <http://www.namibian.com.na/2004/June/national/0449BA231.html

Angelou, Maya. (1986). *All God's Children Need Traveling Shoes*. New York: Random House.

Armah, Ayi Kwei. (1968). *The Beautyful Ones Are Not Yet Born*. Boston: Houghton Mifflin.

Asante, M.K. (1988) *Afrocentricity*. Trenton: Africa World Press.

Bâ, Mariama. (1980). *So Long a Letter*, Oxford: Heinemann Educational Publishing.

_____.(1980). *Une si longue lettre*, Dakar: Nouvelles Editions Africaines.

_____. (1981). 'La fonction politique des littératures africaines écrites', *Ecritures françaises dans le monde* 3-5, 3-7.

Barry, Mariama. (2000) *La petite peule*, Paris: Mazarine.

Baumeister, R and Tice D. (2001). *The Social Dimensions of Sex*, Boston: Allyn and Bacon.

Beauvoir, Simone de. (1949). *Le deuxième sexe*, Paris: Gallimard.

_____. (1953). *The Second Sex*, New York: Alfred A. Knoff.

Beti, Mongo. (1999). *Trop de soleil tue l'amour*, Paris: Julliard.

Beyala, Calixthe. (1987). *C'est le soleil qui m'a brûlé*, Paris: Stock.

Bjornson, Richard. (1986) 'A Bibliography of Cameroonian Literature', *Research in African Literatures* 59: 418-427.

_____. (2001).*The African Quest for Freedom and Identity: Cameroonian Writing and the National Experience*, Indianapolis: Indiana University Press.

Boni, Nazi. (1962).*Crépuscule des temps anciens*, Paris: Présence Africaine, 1962.

Booker, Keith, M. 1998). *The African Novel in English*, Oxford: James curry.

Botwe-Asamoah, Kwame.(2001) 'African literature in European Languages: Implications for a Living Literature.'*Journal of Black Studies* 31.6, 746-763.

Brady, Margaret. (1999). 'Female genital mutilation: Complications and Risk of HIV Transmission', *AIDS Patient Care and STDs* 13,

1-10. Britannica. (2001). *Encyclopedia Britannica*, Chicago: Academic Ed.

Césaire, Aimé. (1968). *Return to My Native Land*, Paris: Présence Africane.

_____.(1983). *Cahier d'un retour au pays natal*, Paris: Présence Africaine.

_____. (1989). *Discours sur le colonialisme*. Paris: Présence Africaine.

Confiant, R et al. (1990). *In Praise of Creoleness*, Baltimore: The John Hopkins University Press.

Conrad, Joseph.(1960) *Heart of Darkness*, Englewood: Prentice-Hall.

Derby, Ron. (2006). 'South African Bride Price Moves from Cattle to Cash', December 17, <http://www.namibian.com.na/2006/December/africa/0662 87285.html

Dharam, Ghai. (1973). Economic *Independence in Africa*. Dar es Salam: East African literature Bureau.

Diop C.A. (1981) *Civilization or Barbarism : An Authentic Anthropology'* Brooklyn: Lawrence Hill.

Dumont, René. (1962). *L'Afrique noire est mal partie*, Paris: Editions du seuil.

_____. (1969). *False Start in Africa*, New York: Frederick A. Praeger Publishers.

Eisler, R. (1995). *Sacred Pleasure: Sex, Myth and the Politics of the Body*, New York: Harper Collins.

Etoke, Nathalie. (2006). 'Writing the Woman's Body in Francophone African Literature: Taxonomy Issues and Challenges,' *Codesria Bulletin*, Nos 3.4, 41-44.

Europe News. (2007). 'Nine French Arrested in Chad for Kidnapping 103 Children, <http://news.monstersandcritics.com/europe/news/articlE_1 368998.php/Nine_French _arrest...

Fanon Frantz. (1963).*The Wretched of the Earth*, 1963. New York: Grove Press.

_____. (1967). *Black Skin, White Masks*, New York: Grove Press.

Gérard, Albert. (1988). 'Oralité, glottophagie, créolisation: Problématique de la littérature africaine', *Bulletin des séances de l'Academie Royals des sciences d'Outre-Mer* 34.2, 259-269.

Greene, Graham. (1959).*It's a Battlefield*, London: Heinemann.

Hamilton, Josh. (1997). 'UN Condemns Female Circumcision', April 19, <http://www. Nbmj.com/content/full/314/7088/1145/g

Hicks, Esther Kremhilde.(1996). *Infibulation: Female Mutilation in Islamic Northeast Africa*, Piscataway: N.J. Transaction Publishers.

Hosken, Fran P. (1980). *Female Sexual Mutilations: The Facts and Proposals for Action*, Lexington: *Women's International Network News*.

Hundley, Tom. (2002). 'Immigrants Bring Practice of Female Circumcision to Europe', *Knight-Ridder/Tribune News Service*, 23-34.

Jambaya, Loveness. (2007). 'South Africa's Virginity Testing', May 22, <http://news.bbc.co.uk/2/hi/africa/667745.stm

Jackson, Hunt, H. (1965). *A Century of Dishonor: The Early Crusade for Indian Reform*, New York: Harper & Row.

Juneja, Om p. (1995) *Post-colonial Novel: Narratives of Colonial Consciousness*, New Delhi: Creative Books.

Kambudzi, A.M. (1998). *Africa's Peace Fiasco: From 1960 to 1995*, Harare: Jongwe Printing and Publishing Company.

Kavulla, Travis. (2008).'Inside Kenya's clumsily rigged

Election', http: January 5,

http://www.cbsnews.com/stories/2008/01/04/opinion/main/367544

King, Martin Luther. (2005). 'Togo: Land of Contrasts', *Africa Today*, 11.8: 22-24.

Klaw, Barbara. (2000). 'Mariama Bâ's Une si longue lettre and Subverting a Mythology of Sex-based Oppression', *Research in African Literatures* 31.2, 133-150.

Koné, Amadou. (1993). *Des textes oraux au roman moderne: étude sur les avatars de la tradition orale dans le roman ouest-africain*, Frankfurt: Verlag fu r Interkulturelle Kommunikation.

Kourouma, Ahmadou. (1970).*Les soleils des indépendances*, Paris: Editions du Seuil.

_____. (1968). *The Suns of Independence*, Trans. Adrian Adams. New York: Africana Publishing Company.

_____. (1990). *Monnè: outrages et défis*, Paris: Editions du Seuil.

Kyoore, Pascal, B.K. (1996). *The African and Caribbean Novel in French*, New York: Peter Lang.

LaFraniere, Sharon.(2005)'Forced to Marry Before Puberty, African Girls Pay Lasting Price', November 27, 2005 <http://www.nytimes.com/2005/11/27/international/africa/27malawi.h

Lewy, Guenter. (2004). 'Were American Indians the Victims of Genocide?' November 22 <http://hnn.us/articles/7302.html

Lightfoot-Klein, Hanny. (1989). *Prisoners of Ritual: An Odyssey into Female Genital Circumcision in Africa*, Binghamton: Harrington Park Press.

Madamombe Itai. (2007).'Combating Zambia's Hidden Hunger.' *Africa Renewal* 20.4, 14-15.

Maino, Eric. (2002.) 'Traditional Circumcision a Health Hazard.' August <http://www.newsfromafrica.org/newsfromafrica/articles/art_849.html

Memmi, Albert. (1965). *The Colonizer and the colonized*, Translated by Howard Greenfield. New York: Orion Press.

Monekosso, Ticky. (2001). 'Africa's Forced Marriages', March 8, 2001 <http://news.bbc.co.uk/2/Africa/1209099.stm

Monga, Celestin. (1997).'Eight Problems with African Politics', Journal of Democracy 8.3, 156-170.

Mosadomi, Tola. (2000). 'Marriage, Women and Tradition in Guillaume Oyono Mbia's Three Suitors: One Husband', *West Africa Review* 2.11-7.

Ngugi, wa Thiong'o. *Petals of Blood*, New York: Dutton, 1977.

_____. (1986). *Decolonising the Mind: The Politics of Language in African Literature*, Portsmouth: Heinemann.

_____. (1989). *Matigari*, Translated from Gikuyu by Waugui wa Goro. Oxford: Heinemann.

Ngwane, G. (2004). 'Cameroon's Democratic Process: Vision 2020' *CODESRIA BULLETIN*, No.3.

Ngwane, Jeff. (2005). 'Corruption is a Plague Affecting Everyone', November 23.
<http://www.postnewsline.com/2005/11/corruption/html

Nyamnjoh, F. (1996). *The Cameroon G.C.E Crisis: A Test of Anglophone Solidarity*, Limbe: Nooremac Press.

Obiechina, Emmanuel. (1975). *Culture, Tradition and Society in the West African Novel*, New York: Cambridge University press, 1975.

Okeyo T.M. (1994). 'Influence of Widow Inheritance on the Epidemiology of AIDS in Africa', Mar- April 1, <http://cbi.mlm.nih.gov/sites/entrez?cmd=Retrieve&db=pub

Okin, Susan Moller. (1999). *Is Multiculturalism Bad for Women?* Princeton: Princeton University Press,

Olaniyan, T. and Quayson, A.(2007).*African Literature: An Anthology of Criticism and Theory*, Oxford: Blackwell.

Orwell, George. (1997). *Animal Farm*, Boston: McDougal Littell.

Oyono-Mbia, Guillaume. (1964) *Three Suitors: One Husband*, Yaoundé: Editions CLE.

Rial, Jacques. (1972). *Littérature camerounaise de langue française*, Lausanne: Payot.

Riesz, Janos. (1991). 'Mariama Bâ's *Une si longue lettre*', *Research in African Literatures* 31.2, 27-42.

Rowell, Andy. (2005). 'Is Nigeria the Next Persian Gulf?' November 10, <http://www.alternet.org/story/27997/

Sa'ah, Randy Joe. (2006). 'Cameroonian Girls Battle Breast Ironing", March 6, <http://news.bbc.co.uk./2/hi/africa/5107360/stm

Sembene Ousmane. (1976). *Xala*, London: Heinemann.

UNICEF. (2008).'Protecting Children from Malaria and Water-borne Diseases', March 17,
<http:www.unicef.org/Mozambique/humanitarian_response-3393.html

UNESCO. (2004). *Educating for a Sustainable Future: Commitments and Partnerships*, Paris: UNESCO.

United Nations Office for the Coordination of Humanitarian Affairs. (2007). 'South Africa: Virginity Testing — Absence of a Small tissue Becomes a Big Issue", July 22,
<http://www.irinnews.or/report.aspx?reportid=56222

Vaiza, Roxy. (2006). 'Breast Ironing in Cameroon: Women in Africa Bear a Painful Tradition.' September 06,
http:// www.theworldy.org/Articles Pages/Artilces2006/September06 Articles/Cameroon-Ironing.html

Walker, Alice and P. Pratibha. (1993). *Warrior Marks: Female Genital Mutilation and the Sexual Binding of Women*, New York: Harcourt.

Walter, Rodney. (1982). How *Europe underdeveloped Africa*, Washington D.C.: Howard University Press. New York: Harcourt.

World Health Organization(WHO).(1994) *Female Genital Mutilation: The Practice*, Geneva: WHO.

Yoder, Carroll.(1991) *White Shadows: A dialectical view of the French African Novel*, Washington, D.C.: Three Continents Press.

www.ingramcontent.com/pod-product-compliance
Lightning Source LLC
Chambersburg PA
CBHW021134300426
44113CB00006B/420